EVANGELISM
MANDATES FOR ACTION

EVANGELISM
MANDATES FOR ACTION
EDITED BY JAMES T. LANEY

HAWTHORN BOOKS, INC.
W. Clement Stone, Publisher
New York

EVANGELISM: MANDATES FOR ACTION

Library of Congress Catalog Card Number: 74-22917
ISBN: 0-8015-2410-5
1 2 3 4 5 6 7 8 9 10

CONTENTS

PREFACE

No word in the lexicon of the church has become more exhausted by use than "evangelism." Yet no word has had richer luster or worthier content.

The Thirty-Eighth Annual Ministers' Week at Emory University took as its theme "Evangelism in the Life of the Church" in an attempt to restore luster and recover content for this central activity of Christian faith. Six speakers brought fresh perspectives and unique strength to this task, and the cumulative impact both of the spoken addresses and of these chapters is to suggest that true evangelism always surprises and startles us by placing our lives in juxtaposition —personally and socially—in such a way that God's creative power in Christ meets us and changes us even as it calls us to disciplined response.

A persistent theme running through these pages is the urgent imperative to relate the individual to his social context even as he is brought into new relation with God. Failure to do this has sentimentalized the gospel, according to the Reverend William Sloane Coffin, chaplain of Yale University and well-known war critic. While less socially specific than Coffin, the Reverend Leighton Ford, associate evangelist with the Billy Graham Crusade, joins in this concern as he reaches toward a holistic approach to evangelism. Dr. Leander Keck, professor of New Testament at Emory, provides biblical and theological perspective for evangelism in his two essays, neatly reversing the usual sequence of expectation with regard to key elements in evangelism. Dr. James May, professor of liturgics and American church history at Emory, helps emancipate evangelism by placing revivalism in historical perspective. The Reverend Tom Skinner, noted black evangelist, ties evangelism and liberation together in a way that requires an appreciation and use of power. The Reverend

James Buskirk brings a depth of personal concern and relationship to his remarks on evangelism in the concluding chapter. Professor Buskirk teaches evangelism at Candler School of Theology.

In their original setting at Glenn Memorial United Methodist Church on the Emory campus, these addresses had genuine evangelistic power. They are offered here to a wider audience in the belief that they retain their power to startle and surprise us while providing suggestive and fresh understandings of the gospel at work in our time.

James T. Laney, Dean
Candler School of Theology
Emory University

EVANGELISM
MANDATES FOR ACTION

CHAPTER 1

EVANGELISM AS SOCIAL PROPHECY

by the Reverend William Sloane Coffin

The Reverend William Sloane Coffin, ordained Presbyterian clergyman, is the chaplain of Yale University. He is a graduate of Phillips Academy in Andover, Massachusetts, and holds the B.A. and B.D. degrees from Yale University. He served as acting chaplain of Phillips Academy and chaplain of Williams College before going to Yale.

1

Christians should know that human unity is not based on agreement but on mutual concern. They should know that when agreement replaces mutual concern as the basis for human unity, disaster strikes. For then the herd mentality takes over. Then slogans become the eleventh commandment on which are hanged all the law and the prophets: "Keep your mouth shut." "Don't climb out on a limb." In the herd mentality men turn the other cheek in order not to see evil. Men hide behind their specialties pleading insufficient knowledge.

I am not an Old Testament prophet; I'm just a New Testament evangelist. Concretely, any man who refused to take a stand, if he believed that American bombing in Indochina was in the name of an offended national pride, was demonstrating a sophisticated version of unsophisticated Cain clubbing his brother to death. It is not agreement, but mutual concern, that is always the basis for human unity. Let me speculate that "Ministers shouldn't meddle in politics" was probably first said not to Martin Luther King, Jr., by Governor George Wallace but by Pharaoh to Moses.

Suppose there were ten righteous men in Sodom and suppose the city wasn't saved because their righteousness wasn't relevant. That would make sense, wouldn't it? Irrelevant righteousness, an incapacity to give priority to what is important, is not only the blood brother of apathy but also the present bane of the church.

Too often we have been concerned with free love and indifferent to free hate. While we have stressed personal morality, we have ignored social morality and run from the giant social issues of the day into the pygmy world of private piety. Too often we have stressed secondary virtues in order to avoid primary virtues. "Woe to you, scribes and Pharisees, hypocrites! for you tithe mint and dill and cummin" — secondary virtues—"and have neglected the weightier matters of the law, justice and mercy and faith . . . You blind guides, straining out a gnat and swallowing a camel!" (Matthew 23:23–24) Why be conscientious if you are only semiconscious of the things about which you are supposed to be conscientious? Secondary virtues must never be stressed at the expense of primary virtues.

Now I am not saying that the church vis-a-vis the nation must at all times and at all places be primarily prophetic. And I am certainly not saying that all ministers should be prophets first and priests second. I take serious exception to those people who say that every minister is supposed to be a prophet and then proceed to make common integrity look like courage. The main reason I object to this idea is that I do not believe it. I do not think everybody is called to be a prophet, and I think it makes an enormous difference whether you are the chaplain of Yale or a parish minister in some rural area of the country.

I am well aware that many of us have gifts of reconciliation. At that point, my only question is, what have you to reconcile? Very often senior pastors with great gifts of reconciliation are not careful enough to make sure they have some fiery young bucks around so there will be something to reconcile.

Once again, I am not saying that all ministers have to be prophets first and priests second.

However, when giant public issues (war and peace, racism, poverty, pollution) so invade the intimacy of every private life that to deny them is to deny part of our own humanity, then not to deal with them is not even to be a good priest, let alone a prophet.

In other words, I think social issues are distinct but not separate from personal issues, particularly in our time. The

Bible very often speaks the same words to both our personal lives and our corporate lives. Just as there is bad news and good news in our personal lives, so there is bad news and good news in our communal lives.

We make a false distinction when we think that evangelism means good news and social prophecy means bad news. I am not even sure that bad news and good news are really that different. That is, in the Bible is it not true that judgment and mercy are ultimately one and the same thing? Judgment for the rich spells mercy for the poor. Judgment for the oppressors spells mercy for the oppressed. Judgment for the United States is merciful for the peoples of Indochina. But more than that, judgment for the rich is, finally, mercy for the rich. Is it not a merciful thing to know that you are not at the mercy of your riches? That there are greater riches with God? Is it not a merciful thing for a nation to know that it does not have to be the richest, the most powerful nation in the world? We don't have to be concerned that our own beloved country must not become a pitiful, impotent giant. We only have to be concerned that it not be a mindless and a heartless one. In the divine dispensation, mercy and judgment are one.

The Old Testament prophets seemed to understand this relationship of judgment to mercy. They first experienced in their own lives and proclaimed the evil that was about to befall their people before it was widely recognized. But at the moment when the onslaught of evil was felt and recognized, these prophets preached the promise of deliverance and redemption.

So it seems evangelism and social prophecy mean that the Bible speaks to our corporate as well as to our individual lives and that in our individual and corporate lives the bad news is an integral part of the good news. Judgment and mercy have met and kissed one another, for God only afflicts the comfortable in order that the afflicted be comforted.

The problem of change

What does the Bible have to say to some of the vexing aspects of life in the United States today? Take the problem of change. No previous generation in America, perhaps in the world, has had to experience such drastic changes. We talk about change very readily. We know change is inevitable, and we ought to know that the art of life is to cooperate gracefully with the inevitable. Yet when it comes to making a change, individuals, institutions, and nations alike resemble the caterpillar which said, looking up at the butterfly, "You'll never find me flying around in one of those crazy things."

At the United Nations not long ago a Latin American diplomat said, "Around here things tend to disappear. If we deal with a small conflict between two small nations, the conflict disappears. If the conflict is between a small nation and a large nation, the small nation disappears. If it's a conflict between two large nations, the United Nations disappears." The United Nations disappears because not one of the great sovereign powers of the world has surrendered to it one iota of sovereign national power. This situation exists in a world that has become a frail planet which can be scuttled at any moment by the dissensions of the crew. We live in a world which can be encircled by an astronaut in an afternoon and, technologically contracted, is no larger than a village. *You'll never find me flying around in one of those crazy things.*

In considering how change affects an institution, we have only to examine our own beloved church. How many times in history has the church mounted the barricades facing the wrong direction! And it is not only the old fogies among us who cannot take change. Believe me, as one who lives among students, the vast majority of them are singing, "For weal or woe, my status is quo."

What has the Bible to say to us concerning this very difficult problem of change? The Dutch theologian-historian Van Leeuwen points out that the four great civilizations of the ancient world—Egypt, Mesopotamia, India, and China— were all static civilizations in at least one respect. The citizens of these civilizations believed in a once-and-for-all ordered creation in which everyone and everything was part and parcel of a sacred order. You didn't play around with it. One cannot visualize Egyptian slaves rising up against Pharaoh, for Pharaoh was believed to be divinely ordained. But then along came the pushy Jews (the language is not Pharaoh's, but mine). These ancient Israelites did not believe in a once-and-for-all ordered creation, but rather in an ordering activity in creation. The God of Abraham, Isaac, and Jacob whom we proclaim as the God of history is, then, a God of change.

Therefore, it should be true for us today, as it was for the ancient Israelites, that one of the worst things you can do in this world is to try to put the freeze on history. This is true in our own personal growth: The senior years should be the formative years. It is true in the growth of our communities, our nation, and the world.

What is the story of the Tower of Babel all about——this tower that was supposed to have its top in heaven——if not an impudent human effort to build a from-here-to-eternity edifice? Predictably, the result was confusion. Confusion always ensues whenever men try to build eternal edifices, either of brick or of ideas. It is wrong for us as preachers to picture for our people an unmoving, immovable, unchanging God high in the heavens who must confront an ever-changing fickle man. It would be far more accurate to picture a constantly moving Spirit of God that is constantly confronting stiff-necked, intractable man.

The great French Jesuit Teilhard de Chardin used to cry out, "God ahead, not God above us." He who goes before us is a cloud or a pillar of fire by night. This moving cloud has a history with a beginning. It has a future, and we must be moving to that future "when it will come to pass in the latter days that the mountain of Zion shall be raised above all the hills and all nations shall flow to it." You know how that story ends.

Christians live in the future more than in the past. We are people of hope more than we are people of memory. It is therefore fair to say that Christians should be permanent revolutionaries. Whether in capitalist, communist, socialist, or any other kind of country, when the social order tries to freeze growth, the Christian has to say no. Justice is a restless norm, and peace has not been achieved for our people.

Why is it that in the U.S. today everybody is saying "Let's go back to Egypt"? Remember when the children of Israel stood on the very borders of the Promised Land after a long, tear-stained trek. They had finally made it. It looked as if they were ready to go in and take over the land. They sent out spies, and when the spies came back there was a majority report and a minority report. The minority report proved once again that a prophetic minority has more to say to a nation than a silent or any other kind of majority. The majority report noted that there were giants in the land "and we seemed as grasshoppers to them." And so we seem to ourselves.

It is always fear that does the people in, isn't it? The opposite of love is not hatred; the opposite of love is fear! This is why we read in the scripture that "perfect love casts out fear." One of the worst features of fear is the way it distorts the truth. Love urges a person to expose himself or herself to the reality of things as they are. While love seeks truth, fear seeks safety. Fear distorts, not by exaggerating the ills of the world, which would be difficult, but by underestimating our ability to deal with these ills. We seem to ourselves "as grasshoppers." Fear seeks safety, and safety lies in failure.

Think of your congregation, think of yourself, think of all of ourselves, think of this nation, and ponder the protective strategy of deliberate failure. How can failure be protective? You can't fall out of bed if you're sleeping on the floor. You can't lose any money if you don't place any bets.

As John Holt has perceptively seen, there is more to the strategy than the idea that you can't fail if you don't try. If you can just think of yourself as a complete and incurable failure, you won't even be tempted to try. If you can feel that fate or bad luck or other people——giants in the land—— made you into a failure, then you won't feel so badly about being one.

And if you can think that the people who are trying to wean you from failure——the Joshuas and the Calebs of this world——are simply trying to use you, then you can stone them with good conscience. This, of course, is exactly what the children of Israel did. On the very borders of the Promised Land they stoned the prophets who said "Go ahead."

Apparently, then, what we most fear is not evil in the world or even the evil in ourselves. We fear the good in ourselves because it would demand so much of us were we to try to realize it. "Go back to Egypt," the cry we hear today, seems to me to reflect a protective strategy of deliberate failure.

One of the great messages of good news that we can proclaim to our people these days is that you don't have to be grasshoppers: You're men; you're women. Isn't it true that we Americans in recent years have learned to fly through the air like birds and swim through the sea like fish? It is time now we walked this land like men.

We preachers should tell people how great they are. How dare you sell yourselves short! How dare you, says the Lord, proclaim that you are a mere grasshopper! Here we stand, not only our own people but the people of the whole blessed planet, on the borders not of the Promised Land but of the *Promised Time* for everybody. Instead of going forward with vigor and determination and hope, we hold back and say, "Let us elect a captain who will lead us back to Egypt."

God is always trying to call people forth from where they are: Moses from Egypt, Amos from the sycamores of Tekoa, Jesus from the carpenter's bench or from his mother, who wanted him to be the best carpenter in town. Now the word of the Lord comes to all of us, calling us from wherever we are to fulfill ourselves, to keep on growing, to become what we were made and meant to be. As individuals, as members of a community, as a nation——in this world we are called upon to humanize the universe and make it fit to live in. To try to put the freeze on history will, in St. Paul's words, "grieve the Holy Spirit."

Now that we have been urged to welcome change, we must be careful. Obviously, all change is not for the good. If there is good news about our own neglected goodness, there is also good news in the Bible about man's sin——if we understand the relationship of bad news to good news.

Our internal bleeding

Let us look at man's sin for a moment. The United States today is symbolized poignantly to me by the woman in the New Testament story of whom we read, "She bled internally for twelve years." After she had seen physician after physician and after she had exhausted all her resources, she was worse rather than better. It seems to me that we are bleeding as a nation, as a people, internally. Unlike the woman, we have not faced up to our bleeding, so we have not sought for the True Physician as she did.

At this point let me digress a bit and cite some of the quack physicians to whom this nation has turned: Dr. Henry Kissinger, whose secret recipe for bleeding is more bleeding, and Dr. Daniel Moynihan, who does not believe in making house calls because the patient is better cured by "benign neglect." I would like to mention in passing, affectionately but still with puzzlement, that great expert in heart transplants, Dr. Billy Graham. I suspect that Dr. Graham takes out one selfish heart and puts in its place another selfish heart. Dr. Graham's message seems to be "Save your soul," whereas I read in the Bible the message "Transcend yourself." Dr. Graham seems to be telling me that I must overcome my selfish impulses, and then he appeals to my selfish impulses. "Invest now, Coffin, and heavenly bonds will pay off handsomely on the other side."

Meanwhile, the nation goes on bleeding. We seem to have developed an incapacity as a people to come to grips with problems that clamor for our attention. We have not been able to contain crime, let alone rehabilitate criminals. The same is true of drugs and addicts. The busing issue is used not to challenge but to nurture our racial prejudice. We cannot seem to come to grips with what we might call the shadow side of national life.

I think the church has a message at this point. Historically, we Americans have been a high-minded people both in our personal lives and in our national life. There is nothing wrong with our ideals; the trouble is in our relationships to those ideals. That is, we tend to try to realize the good by identifying with our ideals and simply repressing anything which does not conform to them.

When I was growing up, I was told that this is the "land of the free and the home of the brave." I believe it is. But in high school nobody stopped to tell me that it is also a country that was founded on the blood of ten million Indians and developed on the sweat of forty million slaves. If I had known that, I could have come to grips with my bleeding. We tend to identify with the good and repress the bad, and so our egos from time to time get inflated by an unjustified identification with our own national ideals. Preachers know the problem. There's a difference between *imitatio Christi* and *identificatio Christi*.

In this respect I think our President is very American. Richard Nixon said in 1971 that the United States is the most generous and most compassionate nation on earth, not only to our people but also to other people. At the military academy he said that U.S. power is solely committed to the service of peace. Now I do not think it is right to say that President Nixon was simply lying or that he is guilty of sanctimonious hypocrisy. It is more accurate to say that he and his hearers are victims of illusions fostered by an incapacity to face what is negative, illusions fostered largely by a church which believes in the power of positive thinking.

At the same time, I am not persuaded that George McGovern was any more aware of the tragic, demonic, distorted, or complicated side of life. Listening to Senator McGovern, one had the impression he really believed that the neighborly act of doing good would be rewarded with victory, that the reality of American experience today reflected the reality of governing American ideals, and that wisdom and generosity would express themselves at the polls. He seemed to feel that all we need is a freshness of spirit when, in fact, the problem may be cancer of the heart. The U.S. electorate was not about to turn out of office the one man who made self-deception possible.

Pastor Neuhaus of New York was close to the truth when he said, "Most Americans will lie to themselves in order not to hate themselves and will hate themselves because they lie." Now there is a description of the diffuse dissatisfaction, the spiritual internal bleeding that characterizes our people. In this connection, I think one has to look at the Indochina war.

The war wasn't started by bad guys. The war was started by good guys who believed in American goodness and thought this goodness might be increased by bestowing it on others. This deception is the subtlest form of imperialism, the most sentimental form of liberalism.

That great theological magazine, the *New Yorker*, picked this idea up when they wrote in August 1972: "When we put forward ideals to cover up self-interested moves, we end by believing in the ideals and letting them entrap us in impossible undertakings—and then, to justify these, we may point with pride to our own self-deception, and maintain that the brutality of our actions is redeemed by the purity of our motives."

I think I have read all the books on Vietnam now, and the best one I have read is *The Quiet American*. It was written in 1954 by Graham Greene, that very shrewd Catholic theologian. In it he concludes that "innocence should wander the world wearing a leper's bell."

The message to the church, and to the nation at this point, is a very simple, straightforward one: In the sullied stream of human life, it is not innocence but holiness which is our only option. Since the words "whole" and "holy" have the same root, the church can proclaim Jesus as the Physician who can make the wounded whole. He can make us whole in our personal life and whole in our corporate life—so that we need not be afraid of the good in us, nor need we fear the bad in us. The vision to which I think we are being called in the future is a vision of wholeness—a vision of holiness.

Violence and nonviolence redefined

The church should not be satisfied with a description of violence in purely physical form. If your heart can go out to St. Peter, lopping off the ear of the high priest, your heart should be able to go out to anybody who is moved to violence because of the sufferings of others. Violence, viewed in this perspective, can be an expression of charity, albeit a distorted one. Apathy can only be the perfection of egoism. It is a delicate question: Which is worse, to have blood on your hands—or water, like Pilate? I believe the church could be much more helpful if it would redefine violence as "that which violates human integrity," and nonviolence as "the determination not to violate the integrity of any human being, beginning with our own integrity."

According to this definition, most of us in the Christian church are exceedingly violent, particularly toward ourselves.

We just love policies of repression. Moralistic terrorism is preached in place of ethical persuasion, instead of bringing out into the full light of day all the ambivalences that are inevitably part of the human equipment. In every relationship of love, there is hate. In every act of altruism, some self-advantage is being sought.

Instead of examining, we repress. These policies of repression are wrong if only because the subconscious has no digestive tract. What goes down has to come up again, and it usually does so in the form of displaced violence. Thus, all the folk who violently repress their sexuality become violent when they see the greater permissiveness of the young. People who repress their ethical natures become violent when others make claims on their conscience. Middle-class youth becomes violent toward middle-class values because it cannot quite take leave of the class it wishes to forswear. Those who repress become, themselves, repressed. The result is disaster. As Freud once observed acidly, it is a good thing men do not love their neighbors as themselves; if they did, they would kill them. That is precisely what we are up against a good deal of the time.

The point is that it is all right to have ambivalent feelings. It is wrong to pretend not to have them. It is wrong, in the sullied stream of human life, to pretend to innocence when, as I suggest, holiness is our only option. It is incredibly ironic that we repress at the same time that we pray to Almighty God, unto whom all hearts are open, all desires known, and from whom no secrets are hidden. I grant you, that is a scary thought. But, if we take it seriously, what is the point of repressing? If we take our theology seriously, why should we try to hide? God's love does not seek values; it creates them. It is not because we have value that we are loved; it is because we love that we have value. So our value does not give us grounds for boasting but only for simple thankfulness.

We don't have to prove anything. We have only to express ourselves. What a world of difference there is between expressing oneself and proving oneself! If we believe in God's love, we believe that the Physician knows us through and through. Then, we have to believe that all is acceptable, and that gets very complicated.

I think St. Augustine was wrong when he said, "I'm glad I'm not responsible for my dreams." Wrong! "Thou shalt love the Lord thy God with all thy heart" means with your consciousness and your unconsciousness, your good instincts and your bad instincts. How are we going to love God with our bad instincts? I think we have to learn to befriend that which is morally intolerable within us in the same way that we would stretch out a hand of compassion toward the lame, the halt, and the blind. Somehow we have to learn to befriend that which we do not like within ourselves. If we don't hate ourselves, it will be much easier to love others. God has a hard time loving those who don't love themselves.

Most people in this country have just enough religion to make themselves miserable. They believe in the confession but not the absolution. It takes more humility to believe in the absolution because that's accepting God's opinion and not your own. Guilt is always the last stronghold of pride.

If we can accept this understanding of violence (that which violates human integrity) and nonviolence (the determination not to violate human integrity) and take it forth into our communal life, we will see that individuals as well as social structures can be outwardly orderly but inwardly violent. And if that is true, and violence means violating human integrity, then without hesitation we who are preachers must call violent any university, business, government agency, or other social structure that condemns human beings to the hopelessness and helplessness of a less-than-human existence. Further, it is clear that those who are concerned with nonviolence must show not only compassion for the victims of violence but also concern for the structures of society that make the victim an object of compassion.

It is at this point that most evangelists are incredibly sentimental. They want to show compassion for the victims of violence while having no concern for the structures of society that make them an object of compassion. This it's-not-serious attitude is sentimentalism of the worst kind. Now this is not to say that we have all the answers. It is one thing to say "Let justice roll down like mighty waters," and something else again to work out an irrigation system. We don't have to be cobblers to know if the shoe fits. What I have experienced in society is that when I say the shoe doesn't fit, the cobblers of America say, "The shoe fits fine; go get yourself a new foot."

Role of the church

We as Christians must point out where human integrity is being violated. For example, there is much talk these days about the blue-collar workers, the ethnics of America. I think they have been grievously violated in spirit. The average factory worker in this country comes home from spirit-mangling labor to a payment on the car, a mortgage on the house, a stultifying television set, an overheated teen-age daughter, and a D-in-English, pot-smoking, car-smashing son. The American dream for him has turned into a nightmare. But has the church ever had the courage and compassion to say to him, "Buddy, you have the wrong dream"? Who ever said that the glories of this world consist of consumer goods?

Has the church ever had the compassion and the courage to go to the factory owner and say, "Look, when you build factories, you know what's good for the machine, but do you know what's good for the men? Have you ever checked them out? Don't sell yourself short, factory owner. You can work something out so that the man who works in your factory does not have to feel helpless, hopeless——as if he had no say in the whole thing. He doesn't have to feel that the wings of his spirit are being clipped all the time."

I don't know what the answers are. I don't think we have to know what the answers are, but if we are serious about our people, serious about the bleeding, we have to be concerned about the structures of our society that are producing these people and this bleeding.

We could examine the violence in the nation toward other people. The United States, like the Soviet Union, has passed from isolationism to interventionism without passing through internationalism. It is high time that the church community said a good word about an international standing army that would rob the United States——and the Soviet Union and China and any other nation——of any moral justification for intervening in the affairs of small countries. We don't know what the answers are, but that is a legitimate concern——to protect a planet which is now a space ship that could be scuttled at any moment by the dissension of the crew.

Here is another example of violence in the world. There are now three billion people on this planet. If you reduce these people proportionately to a town of 1,000, sixty will be Americans, 940 the rest of the world population. Sixty Americans will control half the world population, half the total income. The sixty Americans will enjoy, on an average, fifteen times as much of all material goods as the rest of the citizens. The sixty Americans will enjoy a life expectancy of seventy-one years while the 940, on an average, will be dead by the time they are forty!

Why hasn't the church raised its voice to call for what is long overdue? International income tax, at least. Why hasn't the church recognized, with its understanding of how nations and human beings work, that American foreign aid is giving without receiving? Giving without receiving is downward motion when it comes to nations and very often to individuals. There are many issues of this kind we could raise. But the thing we must remember now is that in raising these issues, in struggling for results, we are struggling in the name of a God who is God of all mankind, in the name of a Physician who heals all the wounded of this world. Therefore, while we struggle with the slave against the master, it is only in the context of a struggle for a world in which there will be no master-slave relationship.

Of course, we must underscore inequality. Even more, we must seek to respect the uniqueness of every man, woman, and child in this world who, in the divine dispensation, is unprecedented, irrepeatable, and indispensable. We must engage in the prophetic criticism necessary to overcome social immobility, but never without the spirit of reconciliation necessary to offset fratricide. We must hate evil, but only because we so love the good.

We must be persuaded, even coerced, by a vision of the future which is given to us in the Bible, given to us in our own hearts. Yet never must we allow that vision to diminish our respect for the range and subtleties of reality. In short, what the church has to say to us as individuals and as "the people" is that we must become twice as tough and twice as tender, as only the truly strong can be tender.

I think it is very right to be a Christian. I do not think Christianity has been tried and found wanting. I think it has been tried and found difficult. It has been watered down again and again, so that Sunday after Sunday throughout the land we perform the miracle of changing the wine into water.

We miss out when we don't recognize how tough it is to be a Christian. The demands of God are not to be taken lightly. We should recognize also, however, that these demands are not without their promises. For instance, is there anything like the sense of integrity that comes with knowing you are in the right fight? Is there anything more comforting than having all your suffering come from without instead of being all torn up within? Or is there anything more comforting than the words, "Lo, I am with you always, even until the end of the age"?

It is a very wintry world outside. Our challenge is to find again that vision and recover those resources that will allow us to live in a wintry world as the first swallow of a new spring.

There is bad news, but there is much more good news. If we take a dark view of the present, it is only because we have such a bright view of the future.

> *"For you shall go out in joy,*
> *and be led forth in peace;*
> *the mountains and the hills before*
> *you*
> *shall break forth into singing,*
> *and all the trees of the field shall*
> *clap their hands.*
> *Instead of the thorn shall come up*
> *the cypress;*
> *instead of the brier shall come*
> *up the myrtle;*
> *and it shall be to the Lord for a*
> *memorial,*
> *for an everlasting sign which*
> *shall not be cut off."*
> (Isaiah 55:12–13, RSV)

Amen.

CHAPTER 2

THE NEW EVANGELISM: WHAT IT MIGHT LEARN FROM THE OLD

by Dr. James W. May

Dr. James W. May is professor of Liturgics and American Church History, Candler School of Theology. He held varied positions before coming to Candler. He is a graduate of Emory University, did some graduate work there and completed his seminary education at Union Theological Seminary in New York. He holds the Ph.D. degree from Columbia University.

2

Most of us assume we know history whether or not we really do. Take, for instance, the following account of John Wesley's Aldersgate experience. My source is a student's examination paper:

> John Wesley had never had a real religious experience. So they had a meeting in Aldersgate Street, and Wesley got converted. I always did believe in street meetings. I think it would be a good thing if we had more street preaching today.

It was some years ago when that young man shared this information with me. I am confident that the intervening years have broadened his historical perspective. At least, I earnestly pray so.

I wish I could claim innocence of extravagant assumptions about our history. Of course, I cannot. But in this day of renewed evangelistic concern in the churches, it is not presumptuous to urge that we ask questions about America's past experiences in sharing the gospel. We cannot back up and start over, even if we want to, and we do not look back to prove a case or confirm a prejudice, but to learn.

It would be neither possible nor helpful to attempt a complete review of the story of evangelism in America. We shall, rather, focus on a single decade. It is a decade reminding us of our own time, in that men sensed the passing of old familiar ways in the church and raised anxious questions about the future. We shall further illuminate these pivotal years by observing the intersection of the careers of two of the more significant evangelists in our history. Then we shall consider a letter which one of these men wrote about the other. It is a letter which raises questions deserving serious reflection.

The pivotal decade is 1825-1835. During these ten years the props were knocked out from under what remained of the old Calvinist system. The nation's religious thought and practice underwent radical reorientation. In the words of a contemporary editor, the church was "almost revolutionized" by what happened. This decade saw the emergence of the pattern of professional mass evangelism that was to remain the dominant model of evangelism until the end of the First World War if not until the present day. Thereafter, the church— that is, the church in the evangelical tradition—would be viewed more exclusively as an agency for evangelism, and the concept of the ministerial office would be revised from that of pastor to that of soul-winner.

Evangelism was by no means a new concern after 1835. The first of the seasons of awakening that have periodically excited the life of the American churches had begun a century earlier. But heretofore, a revival was "a surprising work of God," to be "prayed down," not "worked up." By 1835, however, revivals were no longer miracles but came as men employed correct procedures. When we speak of the "old" and "new" evangelism, in our present context, we shall be contrasting the periods before and after 1835.

A confrontation of giants

This decade saw the confrontation of two of the giants of America's religious history: Lyman Beecher of Boston and Charles Grandson Finney of central New York (which in a real sense was the frontier of New England). Both men were intensely evangelistic, filled with much zeal for the cause of Christ. Yet, beyond this central, unifying loyalty lay vivid and dramatic contrasts. The two represent, respectively, the forces of the old and the new that grappled during the decade in question.

Lyman Beecher was tough-minded, self-confident, and endowed with boundless energy. He studied under Timothy Dwight at Yale, where he saw the grandson of Jonathan

Edwards employing revivals to rout the forces of infidelity and restore the confidence of Christians whipped by the backlash of revolutionary immorality. After Yale, Beecher labored twenty-seven years on Long Island and in Connecticut, defending the faith, building up the church, fighting "Sabbath-breakers, rum-selling, tippling folk, infidels and rough-scuff generally."[1] He distrusted the "lower classes," so often tainted with Jeffersonian republicanism, and he was suspicious of the rich, so often inclined toward Unitarianism or flirting with sundry heterodoxies.

For his evangelistic purposes, Beecher refined the revival as a powerful weapon for assaulting the enemy. His revivals had none of the wildfire set ablaze by the unlettered itinerants operating in the forests and canebreaks of Kentucky and Tennessee. They remained firmly in the minister's hands, true to the Yale tradition. They employed the ordinary means of grace, they balanced preaching with pastoral oversight, and they carefully maintained the purity of doctrine.

So it was hardly unexpected when, in 1826, at the age of 50, Lyman Beecher was called to Boston, the stronghold of the wicked and the headquarters of Unitarianism. Moving his wife and nine children to Hanover Street Church, he at once brought heart to the harried Congregationalists and almost as quickly became the "acknowledged field marshal of New England orthodoxy."[2]

Beecher's confidence had not come easily. Often he had been depressed by the dismal prospects of God's church— bereft of tax funds and other official support (as if the nation no longer really cared) and assaulted by infidelity, Romanism, and barbarism. But now his optimism was firm, bolstered by his faith in the demonstrated power of an aggressive evangelism. America could be persuaded to be Christian. One by one, the unsaved would be brought into the churches. The evangelical churches—i.e., Congregationalists, Presbyterians, and any other Protestants who might come to agree with them—could be tied together in formidable attack on unrighteousness and a mighty, voluntary, benevolent enterprise to redeem the nation. Merchant princes could be persuaded to give their money. The faith once delivered to the saints would be preserved; America would become a Christian nation; and the millennial reign of the Lord would begin.

Yet, even so bold a vision could not suppress all uneasiness. If Americans were to be goaded "along the path of glory,"[3] there must be no eccentric diversions. Beecher thought often of James Davenport, the New England preacher and a Yale graduate, too, who, in the time of Edwards and George Whitefield, went berserk with his visions and trances and riotous ravings, putting new converts to exhorting everywhere, embarrassing the churches, and upsetting the Connecticut legislature. As much as anything else, it was this kind of insanity that put an end to the Great Revival and opened the way for Unitarianism and Universalism in New England. No, God's church could not afford another Davenport!

The second giant figure looming significantly over this decade was Charles Finney. He possessed all the confidence and energy of Beecher, but as to background and temperament, he lived a long journey from Boston and Lyman Beecher.

Finney was seventeen years younger. He was only two when his parents moved from Connecticut to the marches of Oneida County, New York. Sent back to Connecticut for high school, he thought of entering Yale, but friends advised him that there were quicker and cheaper ways of getting what Yale had to offer. So, after a try at teaching school, he ended up reading law in the village of Adams in upper New York State and singing in the choir at the Presbyterian church.

Finney had largely ignored religion until his thirtieth year. The dramatic account of his conversion——his self-conversion, one might call it——is well known. "I will accept [Christ] today or I will die in the attempt," he told himself; and as he sat before the fire in his law office, he was overwhelmed by "a mighty baptism of the Holy Ghost." He accepted "a retainer from the Lord Jesus Christ to plead his cause," and within a few days he had converted almost every sinner in the village.[4]

Friends would have paid his way at Princeton, but Finney declined, certain that Princeton offered only miseducation. He read theology with his pastor, and the Oneida Presbytery, with some reluctance, granted him a license to preach. As the new convert preached in farming hamlets near Lake Ontario, men and women fell from their seats begging for mercy, and others shrieked in agony. "The sword [of the Lord] slew them on the right and on the left."[5] Within six months his credentials as an evangelist seemed established, and ordination was granted. The more orthodox were still skeptical as to Finney's soundness, but he had shown that he could fill the churches. Later he confessed that he had not even read the Westminster Confession before his ordination, but he felt that his teacher understood it. Finney would write his own doctrinal platform. The views that he brought to the pulpit were those of the layman.

Finney moved into the towns along the Erie Canal. He spent twenty days in Rome and gained several hundred converts. Then he preached in Utica and Auburn and Troy. As the new evangelist broadened his area of operations, reports of his meetings raised anxiety among the older ministers. Revivals were not uncommon, but seldom had anyone seen the likes of Brother Finney's. The various innovations that he employed and his vigorous language, a kind not deemed appropriate to the pulpit, were questioned. Even more disturbing was the rash of young preachers, divinity students, and some of Finney's assistants, who, impressed by his "new measures" and exaggerating his eccentricities, moved out to evangelize the surrounding villages. They haughtily rejected the caution urged by older, experienced pastors. Respected ministers, who long had employed revivals of the sort approved by Dwight and Beecher, saw their churches divided by flaming young predicants who urged the "breaking down" or "skinning" of the "unconverted" shepherd of the flock. Older pastors lived in mortal fear of being "skinned."

A letter from Beecher

Meanwhile, in Boston, Lyman Beecher fretted as reports came in of the extravagances in the West. A Boston Unitarian paper printed taunting accounts of happenings in Utica and Troy. Beecher was not attracted by the role of peacemaker, and he did not want to draw further attention to the breach in the ranks of the evangelists. But, as he put it, he was not wont to temporize. So in January of 1827, he wrote to the pastor of the First Presbyterian Church in Troy, Nathaniel Beman, who had invited Finney to his church.* "I can only pour out my thoughts, from my heart, into your bosom, upon such general topics as seem to be in the neighbourhood of danger. . . . I have confidence in the piety and talents of brother Finney," Beecher insisted. "But the more important revivals of religion are, the more should we deprecate all needless repellences. . . ." Beecher's manner was reasonably restrained, though the present-day reader keeps thinking of the pope's condemnation of Martin Luther: "A wild boar has invaded the vineyard." Beecher made no less than eight references to the "indiscretions" of James Davenport. Yet the concluding note was conciliatory: "I believe if brother F. will take counsel, he may be an invaluable blessing."

Here is an intriguing document. Its date falls almost at the midpoint of the three centuries of the evangelistic enterprise in America. It breathes—to use an overworked phrase—of the passionate concern for souls and for the "cause of Christ" which had marked this enterprise from the beginning. Reading the letter, we feel that we stand upon the divide between New England and the American West, between a church system not yet completely freed of its medieval moorings and the modern voluntary system already coming to birth. We sense the anxieties of the defender of the old ways who recognizes the threat of the new. We see reflected the sureness of the new, careless of the old. The new would continue the evangelistic enterprise, but it would be of a different kind.

So let us put our questions to Beecher's letter. What were the perils he saw? How real were they? Did he overlook some? Was he a discerning prophet? What about his own unexamined assumptions? Our questioning may give us insights for our planning today.

We begin with the last question: What were the assumptions underlying Lyman Beecher's commitment to the evangelistic enterprise? We do not read far without learning that Beecher's gospel would shape the nation in the New England

*The Beecher letter is in *Letters of the Rev. Dr. Beecher and Rev. Mr. Nettleton on the "New Measures" in Conducting Revivals of Religion* (New York: G. & C. Carville, 1828).

image. Its church, its ethos, its style, its class structure would mirror the New England way.

For one thing, there would be little of democracy as we think of it. Beecher again recalled the times of Davenport: ". . .laymen and women, indians and negroes, male and female, preached and prayed and exhorted, until confusion itself became confounded." Now that same calamity was threatening the great New England of the West. "Oh, my brother! if a victorious army should overflow and lay us waste, or if a fire should pass over and lay every dwelling in our land in ashes, it would be a blessing to be coveted with thanksgiving, in comparison to the moral desolation of one ungoverned revival of religion." The triumph of the wrong kind of evangelism on the frontier would mark the end of the New England way in America.

If Beecher's social and ecclesiastical views bore the imprint of his times, so was his message conditioned by the intellectual and cultural forces of his day. Till the end of his life he considered himself an orthodox Calvinist, but the Calvinism he espoused had been long since modified by a succession of New England divines. The faith was not only sealed in heaven and delivered to the saints, it was reformulated at Yale and appropriated by Beecher! He affirmed the inspiration of scripture, but for him and his contemporaries the Bible remained a lifeless repository of proof texts. As Horace Bushnell was later to observe, the New England theologians affirmed the revelation of the scriptures, but once they had received the revelation, they thought like rationalists.

Well, we have no right to fault Beecher because he was not as smart as we think we are. But it is appropriate to note that this stalwart opponent of change was himself the product of change. We shall let this zealous evangelist instruct us, however, even when it is to warn us of his own cultural and theological myopia.

Actually, in terms of theology, Beecher and Finney were not too far apart for reconciliation. In his own folksy way, Finney embraced the New Divinity from Yale and employed it as needed to support his preaching. At least there was no theological impediment to a cease-fire arranged between the two in 1828, and three years later Finney was invited to preach in Boston.

Now let us come to Beecher's bill of particulars. Of the fourteen specifications advanced against Finney, seven of them dealt directly with Finney's use of words. Clearly, the style of Finney's language was at issue: his coarseness, bluntness, and indelicacy; epithets violating civilized decorum and Christian courtesy; a harsh and severe mode of addressing sinners——ringing the charges on tavern words like "cursed," "hell," and "damnation."

Remember the importance of words in the revival meetings, not only in the sermon, but in the extensive conversation with sinners on the anxious bench and elsewhere. And don't forget the prayer, which could last for forty-five minutes. Beecher and his like were especially offended by the "prayer of faith," another "new measure" of the western revival preachers, in which the preacher called the name of sinners and supplied details of their depravity. All, said Beecher, in

> Language of unbecoming familiarity with God. . . . Such a thing is possible in good men, but it is piety degenerated and mingled commonly with carnal affection or spiritual pride. A just sense of ourselves and of God, will produce any thing rather than irreverent familiarity. . . . [It] is utterly inadmissible.

What shall we say of all this? Well, some points go to Beecher. Words do misrepresent God. Ministers involved in pastoral care can attest to the significance of words in dealing with emotional crisis. After crediting Beecher with all his points, however, I still believe that Finney's chief sin lay in the injury done to Beecher's New England sense of refinement. Yale alumni just did not use language like that. Even if they did, they would not address upper-class sinners with the same words directed to rough-scuff sinners, especially in a day when "a leveling of all distinctions in society" would be the last step toward "anarchy and absolute destruction."

Another point about language might be helpful. Suppose the definition of the term "language" is expanded to include not only words, but all actions, concepts, images——all media used to convey and receive meaning. Employing this broadened definition, we may include all of Finney's "new measures" in what we might call the new language of evangelism which would predominate in America after 1835. The use of the anxious bench was a new way of communicating, as was praying by women in public. (Beecher said that "female prayer in promiscuous assemblies" is neither commanded nor authorized in scripture; indeed, it is expressly forbidden, "and if we need farther [sic] testimony, the general character of actresses is a standing memorial of the influence of female elocution before public assemblies.")

Finney's very personality—under our expanded definition —was a part of the new language of evangelism. Presumably, if Beecher had seen him in action, his letter would have said much more about this. Finney's compelling magnetism, his thundering voice and dramatic gestures, his searching for effects in every word, his charisma—all this was part of the new language.

In the 1820's, evangelism already was undergoing a language crisis. Or perhaps more accurately, let us say that Beecher was in crisis. He could not envision thousands of unsaved westerners who could not hear him should he speak to them. Finney had no language problem, though later he did develop a rationale for his "new measures." Finney did not need to study the popular mind; he possessed it. And in his own pragmatic way he refined his media of communication.

We cannot dismiss the crisis of evangelism in 1825-1835 as a mere flap over language. Finney's new language of evangelism left some problems untouched and raised a spate of new ones. Uncannily, Beecher's letter, in preliminary fashion, exposed a number of issues which we, with our perspective of a century and a half, can articulate more clearly than he. We shall now examine several of these issues; and if our probing is of necessity superficial, it may at least serve to identify some of the deep problems still requiring attention when we in our own time search for an authentic and effective evangelism.

For one thing, Beecher was much concerned about the pressures exerted upon settled pastors by the enthusiastic young disciples of Finney. What he saw beginning to happen was to continue without abatement until pastors either gave way to the evangelists or reshaped their own work to conform to the model of the new evangelism. Evangelical churches now became evangelistic agencies, and the priorities of ministry were radically revised. Pastoral care, teaching, and administration of the sacraments took second place or fell under total eclipse.

In short, evangelism, extracted from the total ministry of the church, imperially subsumed what remained of the other ministerial offices. The revival even developed its own liturgy which, in the evangelical churches, soon replaced what remained of the classic Reformation services. At worst, the pastor, deemed incapable of the most important work of the church, was reduced to the office of caretaker during the dry seasons between peaks of excitement fostered by the visiting professional evangelist.

Perhaps the chief disaster in the wake of mass evangelism was the failure to explore the obligations of Christian discipleship. The first of Beecher's fourteen charges against the new evangelism was the "hasty recognition of persons as converted upon their own judgment, without interrogation or evidence." His reasoning may seem quaint to our day: Let this continue, he argued, and you will fill the church with hypocrites, and then you will be perpetually agitated by efforts to maintain discipline, or you will be "covered with shame by the neglect of it." Beecher underestimated the threat: By the end of the century the churches had neither discipline nor embarrassment for the lack of it. Third-rate evangelists were comparing tally sheets, figuring the cost per head for the recruitment of new members. One professional, estimating that Dwight L. Moody's converts cost $7.43 apiece, quoted a cut-rate special of $4.92 for the same job.[6]

Conversion was not the beginning of the Christian life; it was the end of evangelizing. Finney, to be sure, compared conversion to baptism. But the new Christian was not engrafted onto the Body of Christ. As the years passed, the convert was merely transferred from the statistical column denominated "prospects" to the column under "decisions."

Ironically, though the church intended to make this country a Christian nation, its sole leverage upon the social order was the personal influence of the individual Christian, and the individual Christian received no enabling assistance toward fulfilling his task. If he looked to the pulpit for guidance, he was told to redouble his efforts at soul-winning. Horace Bushnell's plea for Christian formation within the nurturing community fell upon deaf ears so far as the mainstream of evangelical Christianity was concerned. That so many individual Christians did gain a vision of discipleship beyond the restrictive patterns of conventional piety is hardly attributable to the churches that longed most fervently for seasons of refreshment.

Losing the landmarks

Beecher's letter painted vivid scenes of the desolation to follow in the wake of the new evangelism in the West. Over and over he returned to the motif of desolation:

> By degrees. . .all landmarks will be removed, and what was once regarded as important will be set at nought, and what would once have produced horror will be done fearlessly.

Here we must return to the question about language—language in that larger sense implied by our broadened definition. Language is in itself of indifferent importance. (There is no inherent sacrilege in "Things go better with Jesus" or "Fly the friendly skies of Jesus.") That Finney changed the words—that he adopted "new measures"—does not disturb me as much as it did Beecher. But I must agree with Beecher on the landmarks. This is the question to ask of any "new style" of evangelism: Can you still sight the landmarks? Go ahead; put the fodder on the ground! But can you still see the landmarks?

The "evangelical theology" shaped in response to the popular piety of the revivals, having no roots in the church's traditions, actually encouraged the removal of the landmarks. In his commendable book *Evangelism in the Wesleyan Spirit*, Albert Outler summarizes this removal of the landmarks in nineteenth-century evangelical theology in America. Outler warns against tying the cause of evangelism "to the resurgent residues of nineteenth-century biblicism, supernaturalism, anti-intellectualism, [and] political conservatism. . . ."[7]

Discount Beecher's rhetoric if you need to. Grant that the

differences betwᵤen him and Finney were to a great extent cultural and stylistic. Still, subsequent developments proved his fears justified. Too often the landmarks were removed, making for a church of "empty formalism, bland uniformity, social conformity and political conservatism."

It was all the more difficult to preserve the landmarks because of the anti-intellectualism built into the new evangelism. Beecher foresaw, for instance, the attack on an educated clergy. The new breed of evangelists, he predicted,

> meeting in their career with the most determined opposition from educated ministers, and Colleges, and Seminaries, all these in succession would be denounced, and held up as objects of popular odium, and a host of ardent, inexperienced, impudent young men be poured out. . .to obliterate civilization, and roll back the wheels of time to semi-barbarism.

Again, you may want to set Beecher's rhetoric in the window to cool. But see how uncannily his picture foreshadows the virtual abandonment of the intellectual enterprise in the popular churches. Many an able young person in the nineteenth century felt compelled to choose between being a Christian and using his mind. The churches moved into the ferment of the post—Civil War period incapable of coping with new intellectual currents and relating to the rising corporate structures in our national life. Popular revivals, a bulwark of conservatism, found their escape in postmillennialism and a new pietism hardly to be equated with that of August Hermann Francke and John Wesley. In the South, especially, as Ernest Trice Thompson has pointed out, emerged the concept of a spiritual church, unsullied by contact with life beyond its walls. In it, individual Christians sat firm on their blessed assurance, felt their spiritual pulses, and awaited the Second Coming.[8]

Erosion by imitation

Beecher had already noted what one might call the reckless cocksureness that would mark the evangelistic enterprise. Consider his description of the

> self-sufficient and daring state of mind, which is reckless of consequences, and incorrigible to argument or advice. It

> may be the result of confidence inspired by success; of the
> magnifying effect of intense interest on one subject, which
> throws everything else out of the circumference of vision,
> and into relative insignificance; of nervous excitement. . .
> [or] a settled state of perverted feeling. . .which, in the
> estimation of the subject, becomes absolute knowledge, and
> pours contempt on argument or advice. . . .

This "know-certain-feeling," as Beecher called it, which
increasingly characterized evangelistic activity, has to be
distinguished from the commitment, discipline, and zeal
associated with groups such as the Mormons or Jehovah's
Witnesses or the early Methodist Societies. It was individualistic and idiosyncratic, and notwithstanding the self-inhibi-
tory morality espoused in the revivals, it entailed no criticism
of conventional culture. It thrived in the atmosphere of
success.

We are tempted to see in Beecher's words a description
of the "operator." But I think he was getting at something
else, a tendency, the ultimate expression of which is the
"operator" or the "phony." Let us refer to the tendency as
erosion by imitation. Beecher, as we have noted, was disturbed by the rise, almost overnight, of roving bands of
evangelists imitating Finney's "new measures," but "without
the moral power." Intrigued by the success of Finney's
methods, they hastened to exploit the master's successes.
The ready answer to their critics was: "It works, doesn't it?"
Beecher took exception:

> Though [the measures] may be connected with success, it
> is because God in his mercy works by means of great
> relative imperfection, and not because it is the "more
> excellent way."

To paraphrase Beecher: Whatever might be said of the
presence of God in the new revivals, the imitators, by exaggerating the "great relative imperfections" in Finney's
work, were producing a caricature of evangelism. Uncritical
imitation tends toward caricature, toward exaggeration of
defect and erosion of authenticity.

Finney himself would soon tone down some of the prac-
tices that most offended his critics, bringing his revivals more
in line with those of the eastern seaboard. A fair estimate of

his career credits him with other and more solid achievements than his earlier revivals, the more eccentric characteristics of which were preserved in the preaching of his imitators. Bands of "expert and itinerant tacticians," as they have been called, followed after him and sought to reproduce the experiences of 1825-1835. Before mid-century, however, the revival impulse was dissipated. After the Civil War, the erosion accelerated in the wake of Dwight L. Moody. As he turned toward building up institutions to consolidate the gains of his revival, smaller men seeking to exploit his successes further caricatured both the gospel and the means of presenting it.

One professional revivalist now transformed evangelism into entertainment to compete with P. T. Barnum and the hayseed vaudeville monologist. Mirroring the feelings and aspirations of the white, Anglo-Saxon, middle class, he proclaimed the gospel of success and affirmed the value of church affiliation. Riding a mighty wave of sentiment and nostalgia, he extolled the virtues of "old-time religion." Billy Sunday's tabernacle audiences found excitement and inspiration in his portrayal of religious experiences which they themselves did not really expect to have.

Lessons for today

These, it seems to me, are some of the things we can learn from the American experience in evangelism. We have noted (1) the subtle though profound change it wrought in the concept of the church and its ministry; (2) its failure to explore more fully the obligations of discipleship and to equip the Christian to bear witness in an increasingly complex society; (3) its careless regard of the landmarks of the faith; (4) its failure to cope with intellectual and social change; (5) its spirit of confident self-sufficiency; and (6) its uncritical attempt to exploit success, resulting in the accentuation of its weaknesses and the erosion of its message.

I have cited a tendency toward caricature in the evangelistic enterprise, and I recognize that what I have said is subject to the same charge. Such has not been my intention. Mass evangelism was not a failure. Its positive achievements have been well documented. I have not mentioned the men and women of liberal temper and heroic social witness who, with insights far ahead of their time, sought to free the gospel from the limitations of our partial understanding. Nor could I speak of countless simple folk who, without reference to program or movement or strategy, have shared their faith one with another. Who is so bold as to suggest that the hand of God has not been in all of this?

We give the last word to Lyman Beecher. If, indeed, God's hand has been in these things, "It is because God in his mercy works by means of great relative imperfection, and not because it is the 'more excellent way.'"

NOTES

1. Bernard A. Weisberger, *They Gathered at the River: The Story of the Great Revivalists and Their Impact upon Religion in America* (Boston: Little, Brown and Company, 1958), p. 77.

2. Ibid., p. 81.

3. Ibid., p. 70.

4. Ibid., pp. 91-93.

5. Ibid., p. 99

6. Ibid., p. 240.

7. (Nashville: Tidings, 1971), p. 73.

8. In *The Spirituality of the Church: A Distinctive Doctrine of the Presbyterian Church in the United States* (Richmond: John Knox Press, 1961).

Acknowledgment: Two outstanding sources on the American experience in evangelism are William G. McLoughlin, Jr., *Modern Revivalism* (New York: The Ronald Press, 1959) and Bernard A. Weisberger, *They Gathered at the River* (Boston: Little, Brown and Company, 1958).

CHAPTER 3

EVANGELISM IN THEOLOGICAL PERSPECTIVE

by Dr. Leander E. Keck

Dr. Leander E. Keck is chairman of the Division of Religion of the Graduate School of Emory University and professor of New Testament, Candler School of Theology. Before coming to Atlanta, he taught for thirteen years in the Divinity School, Vanderbilt University. He holds the B.A. degree from Linfield College, the B.D. degree from Andover Newton Theological School, and the Ph.D. from Yale University.

3

To speak of "Evangelism in Theological Perspective" is to bring the gospel to bear on the church's task in the world. This topic is as audacious as it is necessary, for without theological clarity, evangelism degenerates into nothing more than church recruitment——which is essentially what it has become in most congregations.

It is necessary to focus our task. First of all, what it means to bring the gospel to bear on evangelism is not self-evident. Fundamentally, the role of theology must not be confused with providing a theology *for* evangelism. A theology for evangelism belongs to that genre of theological work which is flourishing today——namely, efforts to produce on demand a rationale, a theological justification, for what is self-evident to a clientele. Thus, we are provided with *ex*plicit theologies of sex, of body, of joy, of play, of revolution, along with *im*plicit theologies of law and order, God and country, free enterprise, anticommunism, and technology. Each theology is designed to justify an emphasis, a point of view, or a program of action which is taken for granted, thereby transforming theology into ideology and foreclosing its self-critical function. The theologian himself becomes a propagandist and ideologist for a lobby.

Were one to outline a theology for evangelism, one would select those considerations which buttressed evangelism and would justify again a program and an emphasis for those interested in that sort of thing. The result would probably be reassuring and reinforcing primarily for evangelists. Bringing the gospel to bear on evangelism, on the other hand, means engaging in a critical assessment, allowing the light of the gospel to illumine the evangelism we know so that it can be restructured where necessary. To speak of evangelism in theological perspective is to accept the assignment of engaging in a prophetic act that is critical no less than it is constructive. A significant measure of this prophetic criticism is left implicit, latent, waiting for the reader to make it explicit.

In the second place, evangelism as the church's task in the world also needs clarification, because two extremes must be corrected. One is the view that evangelism stands in the way of the church's task in the world. From this angle, the church's task is seen as humanizing life, as restructuring society, as revolution against every impediment to man's fulfillment; and evangelism is viewed as an obstacle to making life on earth humane because it is concerned centrally with saving souls for heaven. The more souls are saved from this world for the next, the more people are prepared to acquiesce in the status quo. So it is not surprising that both those in power and those without hope of power are hospitable to evangelism. The other extreme holds that saving souls is indeed the true work of the church, that preaching the gospel of personal salvation is precisely what the church's mission is, and that social involvement must come later. If it is otherwise, evangelism becomes diversionary at best and subversive at worst. Both extremes are wrong because they both take for granted the same view of evangelism—namely, that it is the activity which redeems people from this world for heaven. Speaking of evangelism in theological perspective means disavowing both extremes at the outset and reconstituting the subject matter in light of the gospel.

In the third place, it is now evident that we can do this only if we are clear about the gospel. While the gospel is not simply theology preached with fervor, the gospel does include theological convictions and can be clarified only by reflection and criticism. Our task, then, is to discern the gospel theologically so that we may reshape the evangelism we know until it brings truly good news to man as he truly is.

We must first explore the import of the gospel, salvation, persuaded that what the gospel is can best be learned not by defining an essence but by noting its effect. Then, we shall concentrate on the center, Jesus himself. Should our reflections be fruitful, we may find the fulcrum on which one might move evangelism forward so that it will engage the world in which we live, and we might even begin to redeem the evangelist as well.

Part 1-The Contours of Salvation: Apocalyptic Freedom

We begin by reflecting on the phrase "apocalyptic freedom." I would speak of radical freedom were it not for the fact that in our time the word "radical" has been domesticated. Our civilization has absorbed so much violence that the language associated with violence has lost its force. Moreover, both so-called radical politics and radical theology turn out to be rather tame affairs. Given our situation, however, if one were to discern true freedom, he would discover its radicalness as well.

Actually, I am persuaded that the truly radical theology is not the fizzy stuff being hawked today but the old wine of the classical Christian tradition, especially the New Testament. It loses its power, of course, whenever it is transmitted as orthodoxy. Theology always loses its power when its answers are repeated without the questions. I suspect that this is also why the New Testament has become so tame, for we repeat its answers without the questions and so think we agree with it. The New Testament, however, seldom agrees with us.

The New Testament understanding of salvation is shaped by apocalyptic. We do not like this but have come to live with it. We have seen enough premillennialism with its charts and sensational predictions of the end to be able to dismiss it. We have also learned to cope with the discovery that the early church and Jesus himself were apocalyptically oriented. They were wrong in expecting the swift end of the world, and we have come to forgive them for this error in judgment.

We reinforce our patronizing stances by perpetuating a misunderstanding of apocalyptic as starry-eyed otherworldliness, as moral irresponsibility, as bad arithmetic for the oppressed, or as overheated yearning for the Second Coming. Biblical scholarship must assume equal responsibility with premillennialists for perpetuating this misunderstanding. Not until recent years have New Testament scholars such as Ernst Kasemann[1] and theologians associated with the "theology of hope"[2] begun to call attention to the importance of apocalyptic for contemporary theology. It is true, of course, that apocalyptic is not always found in the New Testament in the same way. There is considerable diversity. Our task is not to blend this diversity into a fruit punch theology, but to discern whether apocalyptic does, in fact, illumine our situation and our salvation. I believe we are on the edge of a creative appropriation of apocalyptic as the right mode for theology today.[3]

Apocalyptic must not be equated with the materials it uses. Its materials are indeed an amazing assortment of mind-blowing myths and symbols of beasts, guided tours of the heavenly world, and X-rated descriptions of the agonies of the damned. When fascination with these materials prevents us from hearing what is being said with it all, we no longer recognize that our own situation is being interpreted.

The root issue for apocalyptic theology is whether, in the face of totalitarian evil, God can be counted on, and for what. In other words, the root question concerns salvation and its contours. That is also our question today.

The question of salvation cannot be separated from the perception of man's dilemma. The salvational alternative is always developed in concert with the problem of man. Moreover, a superficial reading of man will evoke only a superficial solution, for the answer never goes deeper than the dilemma. The power of apocalyptic theology lies in the fact that it probes the depths of the situation. Because it speaks of radical evil, it also speaks of radical salvation as the liberation of the whole world.

To speak of the liberation of the world requires us to see its bondage. We have become aware of the multiple forms of bondage because minority groups in our country have forced us to see what we have done to them. It is no surprise that black theology has emphasized liberation as its dominant theme, a liberation which cannot be limited to freeing the individual spirit so that external bondage is tolerable. Rather it is a liberation which includes the freedom of the whole man and the whole community to determine their identity and destiny. Furthermore, we have been made aware of the bondage in which the Third World sees itself: the bondage of economic exploitation by Western nations, bondage to disease and poverty, and bondage to its own oligarchies of power. It is perfectly understandable that the rising theologians of the Third World should insist on a theology which does not foreclose revolution but which may even insist on it.[4]

The point is that the gospel liberates men from the bondage they know best, or it does not liberate them at all. We whites who participate in middle-class structures of power should refrain from criticizing the theologies of those who seek emancipation from us, if for no other reason than because such a critique will always be seen as an attempt to turn back the challenge to the status quo. In any case, we must discern our own bondage and cope with that. It may turn out that once we probe this bondage deeply enough, what we find will pertain not only to middle-class whites but to all men.

The search for salvation

We now ask whether or not apocalyptic theology, as it is being offered today, helps us to assess the salvation of persons. Traditionally, the gospel has been addressed to individuals. A hallmark of Protestant Christianity is its insistence that faith and salvation be appropriated by personal decision in response to the preached word.

But who is the person? Apocalyptic theology exposes the inadequacy of both the personal salvation offered by traditional evangelism and the salvation sought by contemporary mentality. Traditional salvation is inadequate because it separates the guilty self from society, while the current quest for salvation separates guilty society from the self.

Much traditional evangelism assumes that man is a self-contained being who has relationships to other persons and to society and that these relationships are essentially external to the sinful self. The self is not really shaped by these relationships. This assumption is why traditional evangelism saves souls first and then asks the saved to change relationships and structures afterward. This is why repentance is distorted into individual regret for not being religious sooner. Actually, however, the self does not have social relationships but is itself shaped by social relations. The only self I know is a social self, a transcending center of a network of relationships to others and to my culture. The self is a part of Adam, the composite symbol of man in the Old Age. To save this self is to redeem and heal this network of relationships. This is why repentance cannot be simply individual remorse; it must include a social reconstruction. Because our guilt cannot be restricted to personal sins but must be seen as our participation in the ubiquitous sin of the whole creation, salvation cannot be restricted to what transpires in the individual soul but must include the transformation of the network of relationships which makes us who we really are.

The popular alternative is equally naive at a different point. This modern alternative seeks salvation for the individual by liberating an innocent self from a guilty society. The demand is for individual authenticity by freeing the self. Is the self that is liberated from cultural constraints really authentic, though? Is it a good self? What understanding of man is this which assumes that removing psychological inhibitions or cultural mores with regard to sex or speech or societal structures will free a self that ought to be fulfilled? Fundamentally, this view of mankind asserts that the individual is essentially an innocent victim of repressive structures imposed by others. It is essentially a romantic view of man, one which can be traced at least as far back as Rousseau's view of the happy and noble savage. It is also the ultimate self-delusion.

Let me be clear. It is undeniable that individuals today are victimized by oppressive structures, whether it is male chauvinism, assembly-line education, or outmoded mores with regard to our bodies. Victimization is not disputed. What is disputed is whether or not the victimized individual is innocent. If he is innocent, then he will achieve his salvation when the coercive structures are removed so that he can fulfill himself. If he is not innocent, then the liberated self will fulfill precisely what it really is——a guilty accomplice in its bondage.

It is useful to pursue this idea by commenting on a recent interpretation of man's salvation in which the classical Christian view of man is largely absent. I refer to Gustave Todrank's book, *The Secular Search for a New Christ*.[5] I use Todrank simply because he exemplifies a mind-set of the day, not because his book is especially important in itself. Todrank is convinced that a revolution is under way in Christianity. He sees a trend toward theology without God, Christology without Jesus, the Bible without authority, a church without clergy, salvation and morality without immortality. His perception of the trend is accurate enough. What concerns us here is his understanding of salvation, because he himself asserts that "the point at which the obsolescence of traditional Christian theology is most evident is in its scheme of salvation." (p. 28)

It soon becomes evident that he, too, has in mind an essentially individual salvation. When he defines salvation as "that total life orientation which makes for the most and the best creative well-being" (pp. 46-47), it is clear that his is a middle-class view of man, for whom salvation is the good life in the here and now, marked by continuing self-actualization. His call for cooperation among men (p. 45) does not really open up the social character of existence. This individualistic, entrepreneurial salvation is manifest also when he speaks of the need for luck and comments that "as man's knowledge increases he will be able to eliminate much of the risk and improve the chance for good fortune, but for the present we must acknowledge both risk and luck, and that some are luckier than others." (p. 48)

He rejects all claims that Jesus is the only saving agent and says, "Each individual and group must be given the opportunity and responsibility to discern for itself what constitutes its noblest fulfillment, keeping in mind the legitimate claims of the larger community." (p. 71) Here there is no judgment on our aspirations. They are presumed to be good and legitimate precisely as they stand, needing to be limited only where they impinge on the aspirations of others, somewhat as competition is to be regulated in a free market. One cannot help but wonder how the "legitimate claims of the larger community" are to be determined, and how one will cope with the pressure to disregard them in order to achieve fulfillment for oneself and his tribe. After Auschwitz and Vietnam, such a view has lost its credibility.

What has Todrank to say about guilt? He defines evil as "those aspects of the environment which in fact resist creative ordering and hence become obstacles to the better life." He regards it as "reasonable to assume that God is doing everything possible to reduce and eliminate evil in the world." (p. 150) Hence, man should help. "The best possible solution to evil is total commitment to the process of salvation." (p. 151) Only after this is said does he turn to that ugly theme, sin.

Actually, it is not very ugly, for he sees it as a voluntary act.

> . . .the sinner must be in a position to acknowledge two or more possible ways of thought and action, and these alternatives must be acknowledged as of unequal value. Sin assumes that the sinner deliberately sets aside his commitments of the past, that he chooses short-range benefits over long-range ambitions, and that he flouts his own inner sensitivities and integrity for an incoherent and self-destructive path of behavior. The puzzling thing is whether anyone would behave in such a fashion unless he was psychologically ill. If he is ill, to what extent does the moral responsibility that is usually associated with sin apply? (p. 152)

If only man's dilemma were so simple as a deliberate wrong choice! Todrank shows no awareness of our propensity to veil the character of our deeds from ourselves, to rationalize the most vicious deeds in the name of the noblest ends, as Vietnam makes unforgettably clear.

He goes on to speak of "the inner turmoil and tension associated with feelings of guilt, the depression associated with failure and the insecurity of not knowing for certain whether the condition can be corrected for good." But this too is a middle-class view of man as the success-oriented creature who engenders psychic difficulties on the way to achievement. Unfortunately, the problem of guilt is not merely a matter of our feelings, for just as we usually sin without feeling guilty, so we can also feel guilt for imaginary sins, as every counselor knows. When Todrank limits repentance, which he defines as regret, to "the initial phases of salvation," he assumes that sin is something we outgrow as we become more successful in the quest for fulfillment.

This is why he can say that "a christ is any personal agent who recognizes another's inability to achieve his desired goal and acts instrumentally to that end. A satan, in contrast, is a personal agent who deliberately manipulates his victim into his nefarious ways, unconcerned about the inner turmoil that is certain to result." Had Todrank pondered this last statement, he might have seen that he actually stumbled into reality——the reality that, by his own definition, shows each of us to be more a satan than a christ. We manifest our bondage by the fact that we do not scheme to do satanic acts but do them because we are enmeshed in a satanic pattern which blinds us to what we are doing. We are sinners before we sin. In a word, because Todrank has bypassed Marx and Freud, what he offers is really an eighteenth-century view of man. In the twentieth century, however, this view should no longer be taken seriously, even if it is popular today.

The vision of apocalyptic

After seeing this kind of pop theology, the depth and scope of apocalyptic theology is evident. We cannot outline here a comprehensive sketch of apocalpytic.[6] We must be content with some general observations and brief comment on two motifs which are fundamental to both apocalyptic and to our present situation.

One of the motifs which gives shape to apocalyptic theology is the drive to see things as a whole, to reduce complexities to fundamental images and perceptions. For example, the entire history of man is seen under the rubric "this age" in contrast with the "age to come." We must distinguish this periodization from our habit of dividing history into categories such as the Ice Age, the Bronze Age, the Dark Ages.

When apocalyptic speaks of this age and the age to come, it contrasts the whole of history with the future which God shall bring. Apocalyptic does not deny historical changes. It insists that despite them there is a fundamental continuity, a pervasive quality, which marks the whole and sets it apart from the age to come. The real future, the radical future, is not what is yet to happen within history;[7] it is the alternative to history seen as a whole. The radical future is not the outgrowth of the present but God's answer to our history. For Paul, our total history can be symbolized by Adam, and God's radical future by the New Adam.

This dualism is also qualitative, because for apocalyptic theology this age is marked by bondage. History is in the grasp of powers which are opposed to God. Moreover, human history is only part of the picture, for the whole creation is in bondage to malign powers. Apocalyptic theology does not separate man from nature. It sees the whole creation as subjected to tyranny, to usurping powers, with the result that neither history nor human activity can develop organically into the kingdom of God. Further, because apocalyptic insists that God is faithful to himself and to his creation, apocalyptic asserts the eventual vindication of God. The godhood of God will manifest itself in the transforming of all creation, not in fulfilling its present potential. Fulfilling the present means that both wheat and tares grow, that every increase in good is accompanied by a growth of evil as well. Thus, the fulfilling of the present potentiality does not really change the character of things. For the apocalyptist, it is a false hope to expect the wheat to crowd out the tares with the passing of time.

The third underlying conviction is that in the midst of history there exists a community that is out of step because it lives by the real future. It is by no means immune from the vicissitudes of history; rather, it is vulnerable to all the conditions of this age and so struggles to be faithful. Nonetheless, it lives by the pledge of the real future and thus has a foretaste of that future by faith. For the Christian apocalyptist, the basis of this anticipation is Jesus and his resurrection, which is regarded as the curtain-raiser of the New Age.

For Paul, Christians live in a tension between the "already" and the "not yet," between what is experienced of the New Age now and what is yet to come. In the case of the fourth gospel, this tension is greatly reduced because for the believer the decisive thing happens in believing. The more John emphasizes this idea, however, the less he is able to speak of the redemption of the world. On the other hand, because Paul keeps this tension, he writes of the forthcoming redemption of the creation. In our day, I believe Paul to be the more adequate, because for him the salvation of men and the redemption of creation coincide, and both are God's future. In the meantime, we live by trusting the vindicating rectitude of God; and we are never satisfied with the present but are always changing it because the image of the future will not let us go. For the moment I shall concentrate on Paul, recognizing that he is neither the whole of the New Testament nor the whole of the truth.

The radical future

According to I Corinthians 15, the coming of the radical future is marked by three stages. First is the event of Jesus and his resurrection, which shifts the balance of power and so makes possible a new kind of existence ahead of time. The second stage, the one in which Christians live, is understood as the reign of Christ during which his power is pitted against the principalities and powers which dominate the present age. The third stage is the end, in which the powers are defeated and the kingdom is handed over to God. This mythological scheme deserves to be taken seriously, though not literally. That is, it is a narrative framework which clarifies who we are in our world and what we may hope for from God.

According to I Corinthians 15, the ultimate enemy is death, and according to Romans 8, all creation is in bondage to futility and decay.[8] For Paul, the mortality of every living thing is a theological problem because death is the opposite of life. Since God is the author of life, the fact that everything which lives must die suggests that life is subject to a tyranny which intrudes into what the Creator has made. Death, as Paul sees it, is not a neutral fact but a hostile power who contends with life and hence with the source of life. The book of Genesis suggests to him that bondage to death is tragic because God did not create us for death but for life. For Paul, this bondage is the result of sin.

The connection of sin and death is not peculiar to Paul and the apocalyptists; however, the manner in which they relate the two is unique. Paul does not say that men sin because they are mortal, but that they are mortal because they sin. The myth of the Fall is not an attempt to excuse ourselves by blaming poor old Adam; rather, it is a way of saying that we cannot blame this mess we are in on creation and say, with Todrank, that this is the best God has been able to do so far. The myth of the Fall asserts our solidarity with all creation and its mortality, as well as mankind's responsibility. Mankind has brought death upon creation and so lives in a bondage which is tragic but neither original nor final. What this theology is saying is that the bondage to death is not mankind's ultimate destiny——for God will not be effectively God until death is overcome——and that even now God is battling against death.

It is not difficult to see that Paul is right: death is the usurper who tyrannizes us in the world. No civilization has worked harder at denying this fact than has our own. Not only are we obsessed by the passion to remain perpetually youthful and so forestall death, but we even deny people the right to face their own death. And once they have died, we conspire to hide the fact from the bereaved. Our passion for life is really a symptom of our fear of death. But if the fear of death is the dominant fear, then we are truly in bondage to death.

Moreover, we have come to the point where we worship death. It has been said that where God is dead, there death is god. Be that as it may, there are numerous indicators that death is what we worship, that it is to death we offer ourselves and our world in order to buy more life. Only in recent years have we come to see that we have killed our forests and valleys, our wildlife and streams, in order to prosper our lives. Nor did we shrink from genocide as the price of our life, for we persuaded ourselves that the only good Indian is a dead Indian. We were so convincing that today the surviving Indians are saying so, too, just as their bumper stickers proclaim the truth that "Custer died for your sins." In Vietnam we were prepared to slaughter a people in order to save ourselves from communism, and we regarded the daily body-count as a necessary sacrifice to death.

Wherever we acknowledge that the death of nature and the death of other people is a fair price for our life, we manifest our worship of death as the evil god to whom we are beholden, as the reality we must satisfy in order to thrive, as the power who has the decisive word over us. In our common mythology, we expect death to be the destiny of our world, either by abrupt nuclear nemesis or by slow suffocation or starvation. We accept universal death as the destiny of our planet because we are not all persuaded that in the long run mankind can really change the rush of events. In a way, we have appropriated the apocalyptic understanding of the world without the apocalyptic understanding of God.

The gospel, however, is the promise of apocalyptic freedom from death, the ultimate enemy. It is the radical pledge that death does not have the last word and, therefore, must not be worshiped. The gospel does not call simply for a reconsideration of the evidence (such as the promise of new technological advance) or for a shift in point of view (that nature dies but man is immortal in any case). Nor does the gospel according to Paul settle for an existential salvation in which deciding selves come to authentic existence over against nature. Existentialist theology assumes that man's true existence separates him from the world of things; thus, Bultmann holds that when a person decides for God, he necessarily decides against the world. It apparently never occurs to him that in deciding for God one decides for the world. But that is what Romans 8 means.

The apocalyptic vision of the destruction of death, of either a renewed earth or of a new creation, must not be taken as pseudoscience, as a literal prediction that there will be a time when leaves will no longer fall, when birds and men will live and multiply forever. Rather, it is a theological myth which expresses our refusal to consign everything to death. It expresses the conviction that the final reality has to do with life, that beyond death is resurrection and transformation. In the name of this myth we resist the tyranny of death, for the struggle against death reveals not only who we are but also who God is. Apocalyptic freedom from death affirms that the ultimate mystery which surrounds us and shapes us is life and life-giving and that this mystery can be counted on in the face of death. If this be true, then every resistance to death is a blow for the freedom of the world. Given the tyranny of death, salvation today means the freedom to say no to death in all its forms. An evangelism that saves souls but leaves men in fear of this manifold death is really a pseudosalvation.

According to I Corinthians 15, the ultimate enemy is death, but the penultimate enemy is the totalitarian rule of principalities and powers. These are the governing forces of history and of man's institutions. They are the intangible realities at work through social structures and movements. They operate in diverse ways, whether in the mind-set of a culture or as demonic forces which pervert the good. This, too, is a highly mythological way of understanding civilization. But once we stop trivializing it by thinking of gremlins, we discover that it merits our serious attention, for this mythological motif shows us the totalitarian character of our civilization.

That our civilization is increasingly totalitarian is becoming apparent to many persons.[9] Totalitarianism is a many-sided word. It does not mean simply fascism or communism. It refers to the fact that government is involved in the total life of the citizen and of the entire nation, so that nothing remains unaffected by the power of the state. It now appears inevitable that governments of large technological societies, including our own, are totalitarian. The more complex our society becomes and the deeper its problems penetrate, the more evident it seems that only government has the capacity to deal with these problems.

It is not only the sheer size of government that can no longer be controlled. The scope of its activities cannot be checked either. Today, it is virtually impossible to think of an area of life which government does not touch. Worst of all, government uses its vast power to increase its power. In order to maintain the system, our army spies on civilians and the FBI spies on Congress. With regard to the war in Vietnam, the government told us everything but the truth in order to get us to consent. Government manipulates the flow of information as well as the flow of funds in order to seduce us into agreement. We are heirs of what J. L. Talmon calls "totalitarian democracy," which he traces to the eighteenth century and the French Revolution.[10] It was then, he shows, that politics came to embrace the whole of human life and that resistance was regarded as betrayal of the people themselves.

It is important to see that this situation is not the result of some conspirator who plotted and manipulated our civilization so as to create the superstate. Rather, there are forces at work which sweep us along. No one planned the present elephantiasis of government. No one planned for us to become embroiled in a war which would bring us to the brink of ruin. Many factors are at work, such as the cold war and the need to rely on government to correct injustices to minorities and to guarantee a minimum standard of living. In all this, we ourselves have a responsibility, for we all expect the government to "do something" whenever a problem is identified. In the hope of servicing ourselves, we have helped to create a supermonster which no longer serves us but manipulates us. We are accomplices in our own bondage.

Now Paul speaks of principalities and powers, of the rulers of this age. Thereby he blends the Hellenistic mythology of heavenly powers who dominate the earth with Jewish apocalyptic which speaks of the two ages. This strange mythology attempts to understand the same sort of phenomena we have been talking about——that there are intangible forces at work, shaping even the shapers of history. Moreover, because apocalyptic emerged in the time when Jews confronted a government which proclaimed itself the divine economy for the whole civilized world, they discovered the demonic element in political power. Today, also, apocalyptic discloses the demonic element in the pretentiousness of the state and of its tacit claim to be the savior of men.

Apocalyptic understanding of freedom, however, can emancipate us. Apocalyptic denies that any existing government, or any revolution against it, can provide a decisive alternative to the totalitarian quality of the state. This insight does not mean that no change is worth the effort or that all political action is futile, for this would also turn out to be a worship of the state. Politics does change things, and sometimes for the better, as the struggle for the rights of minorities shows. The point is that apocalyptic teaches us not to take at face value all the claims and promises that are made. In other words, apocalyptic debunks the pretensions of the established order and revolutionary movement alike, thereby freeing us from false expectation and false worship. Against every claim to be or become the movement into the kingdom of God, it speaks its "not yet." At the same time, against all despair and acquiescence, its "already" rouses us to whatever action may be possible in a given situation, at least to the possibility of disbelief.

This "already" is grounded in the event of Jesus and his resurrection. Because it was in the name of the political status quo that Jesus was executed, his resurrection means the denial of the status quo and of the state's claim to have the last word. As William Stringfellow put it, "Resurrection is verified when rebellion against the demonic thrives."[11] To say that Jesus is Lord is to subvert the claims of every state and political program vying for our ultimate allegiance.

Apocalyptic helps us to cope with the fact that today everything has become political. Whoever says that the gospel must stay out of politics says, in effect, that the gospel is irrelevant to everything. Apocalyptic shows us that this pervasive politicization is not the way of salvation but is precisely the demonic force from which we need freedom, the freedom to engage in politics without illusions.[12] Just as in New Testament times apocalyptic freedom "desacralized" the cosmos, showing it to be a thing and not a divine system, so in our time apocalyptic shows us that our task is to desacralize the state.

Freedom from bondage

We appear to have wandered off the trail somewhere, and you may be wondering what all this has to do with evangelism. Actually, we have been exploring a way of understanding salvation in our time, and salvation is, I take it, what evangelism is all about. We have been asking if a reconsideration of apocalyptic theology helps us to speak news that is really good, if there is any freedom from the bondage that marks our time. If the gospel does not bring freedom where we need it most, then it is reduced to an opiate of the people, nothing more than a Jesus-trip.

The point is that today salvation means the freedom to say no to the pretensions of the superstate and to the tyranny of death. And it means to say yes to human needs in the name of that future freedom which is in the hands of God and which he has pledged to us. In our time it may be more necessary to say no first. Otherwise, we shall be sucked into saying yes to the status quo and its future, and that is not the kingdom of God despite its claims.

Perhaps the situation which I have emphasized does not agree with what others take it to be, and some will not find apocalyptic freedom to be as viable as I believe it is. This disagreement does not matter, for in our pluralistic time there will be various perceptions of man and diverse modes of salvation. What matters is whether or not the apocalyptic perception sees clearly and deeply enough what it does see. To deal with that question is precisely what it means to engage in theological reflection about the good news, precisely what it means to speak about evangelism in theological perspective. When we all begin to do that, as seriously as we know how, we may yet discover the contours of real salvation. Then we will be able to share this discovery with the world.

Part 2-The Flesh Becomes Word

The Christian gospel has its center in Jesus. But we need to ask whether our presentation of Jesus does justice to him or obscures him. This is the central task of Christology, the understanding of Jesus the Christ.

The title of this section is not a misprint. I have deliberately inverted the famous phrase in John's gospel that in Jesus "the Word became flesh." I do not mean to suggest that John should be corrected. I do suggest, however, that saying "the Flesh becomes word" can have the same function for us that saying "the Word became flesh" had for John.

So we have our agenda. The first item is to explore the function of the incarnation in John. The next item calls for us to ask how John's understanding of Jesus comports with the Jesus of history. Finally, we must ask how the Flesh, the historical Jesus, becomes word.

Function of the incarnation

"And the Word became flesh and dwelt among us, full of grace and truth; we have beheld his glory. . . ." (John 1:14) Why does the gospel of John make such a claim, and what is its function in the gospel as a whole? It is too simple to aver that John says this because it is true, since other parts of the New Testament also claim to speak the truth about Jesus but do not speak of incarnation. The synoptic gospels say nothing about it: Matthew and Luke speak of the Virgin Birth, and Mark does not mention Jesus' origin. It was the later church which combined these synoptics to say that the Word became flesh in the womb of the Virgin Mary. No one in the New Testament says this. So the later harmonization is not a good guide to the New Testament itself. But there must be a reason why John insists on the incarnation of the Word.

It is not necessary to discuss the history of the idea of the Word, Logos, to decide whether John depends on some strand of Judaism or of Hellenism. Nor is it necessary to discuss the history of the text of John so as to determine when the prologue was added, or to discuss the development of the prologue itself so as to determine whether or not John 1:14 was always part of this hymn. Our task is to see what is gained by John's making this claim of the incarnation at the beginning. The incarnation of the Word, the Logos, is never mentioned again in this gospel. But because John asserts it in the prologue, the incarnation is assumed throughout the narrative which follows. John wants us to understand the whole story as an account of the incarnated Logos among men.

The Johannine prologue ends with the assertion, "No one has ever seen God; the only Son, who is in the bosom of the Father, he has made him known." (John 1:18) We can translate the last clause as "he has 'exegeted' him." That is, Jesus interprets God because he is the incarnate Son or Logos. At the beginning, the prologue says that the Logos is the Creator. This means that in dealing with Jesus, we have to deal with the Creator, who was among us as a creature. For John, meeting Jesus is infinitely more than meeting a highly original and profound teacher from Nazareth; to meet Jesus and his claim is to confront the Creator. The response to Jesus has ultimate consequences, for there is no way that one can trump a confrontation with his own creator.

This confrontation and its consequences form the theme of John's gospel. Although the Light has come into the world, "Men loved darkness rather than light because their deeds were evil." (John 3:19) Because in rejecting Jesus, men reject their Creator, John says that "he who does not believe is condemned already," whereas he who believes "does not come into judgment but has passed from death to life." (John 5:24) That is, the definitive judgment which apocalyptic theology places in the future, at the so-called Second Coming, John places in the encounter with Jesus now. The ultimate verdict occurs when one responds to him.

This idea is the reason John presents Jesus' encounter with the Jews the way he does. J. Louis Martyn has shown that John's portrait of this encounter reflects the growing bitterness between church and synagogue.[13] Bultmann and others, however, are also correct in saying that, in many passages, the Jews stand for the world. In any case, we must not read the Johannine stories of Jesus and the Jews as actual historical descriptions of what passed between them. It is virtually impossible that the historical Jesus himself ever said his fellow Jews were of the devil (John 8:44). John has Jesus say such things to make concrete the ultimate issues, the real crisis, which is exposed when anyone rejects Jesus. For John it is a matter of light and darkness, life or death, God or Satan. Because Jesus is the incarnated Creator, those who accept him receive the ultimate——eternal life——while those who repudiate him condemn themselves. The story of Jesus and the Jews is written to show this.

From John's point of view, the ultimate character of one's decision with respect to Jesus can be exposed only if Jesus is the Creator and not merely a spokesman for him. What Jesus is able to do for man depends on who Jesus is. This is why the debates with the Jews (the world) repeatedly turn on the question of who Jesus really is. For this reason also, a saving faith centers on believing that Jesus is the Son from the Father. In effect, there is no salvation without believing a particular Christology.[14] Here we have one of the most dangerous aspects of the fourth gospel, for it has suggested to later times that believing dogmas is what saves.

John takes this absolutist either/or position because of his dualism, not a dualism between matter and spirit but between the realm where the Spirit holds sway and the realm of the perverted creation, which he calls flesh. "That which is born of flesh is flesh, and that which is born of Spirit is spirit." (John 3:6) Nothing less than a total rupture with the world of flesh and sin and Satan, nothing less than having a new Father, nothing less than being born again will suffice. To be of this world or to be of the Father——that is the alternative. What is of this world cannot translate us to being of the Father, because this world prefers darkness to light. Only an outsider who is not of this world can break us out of it. This is why Jesus is *in* the world but not *of* it, and why the believers are also forbidden to be of it while they remain in it. John speaks of Jesus as the outsider who momentarily becomes flesh without being of the flesh, because this is the only way that men can be rescued from being of the world.

John's answer fits the problem as he sees it. The more radically one sees the situation of man, the more radically different from the world the Savior must be. At the same time, the Savior must identify with men, for an apparition from another world cannot break us out of bondage. In short, for John the Savior must be God in order to *save* men and be man in order to save *men*.

But what if one does not see the problem of man as John sees it? Then John's Christology is inappropriate; and his theology is an answer to a question that is not being asked. This is clear if we look at the other gospels. For instance, the root problem for Matthew is that men do not do the righteousness which God requires. The Pharisees know the law but do not do it. Or they observe the details but miss the heart of the matter, real righteousness and mercy. So Matthew's Jesus is the one who by word and by deed clarifies what man must do, and who, by calling men to follow him, enables them to begin walking in the way of righteousness.

But in Matthew, the verdict on one's life comes only at the end of history, not at the time of the decision to believe. What is inconceivable to John is what Matthew insists on—that at the end there will be surprises for believers because those who said "Lord, Lord" but did not do what was required will be dismissed; while those who did what was required will be welcomed even though they did not say, "Lord, Lord" at all. John's eschatology reassures the elect; Matthew's deprives them of their security. Because Matthew does not see man's need as liberation from being *of* this world, he does not need incarnation. Given his perception of the human situation, incarnation would have been a case of theological overkill. It is enough for him that Jesus was Son of God from conception onward; that suffices to show that Jesus did not earn the right to be Son of God or learn what God's will is, but was God's man from the outset.

I have outlined the Christology of John to show why he begins his gospel from above, in the heavenly world, rather than from below, in history, where Matthew began. John sees the whole cosmos in bondage to Satan and sees men as slaves who do not even know that they are slaves. So he is convinced that only a savior who is not at all *of* this world is capable of exposing that slavery and of breaking men out of it as well. Thus he begins from above, with the Word who became flesh.

Now we understand why the content of John's gospel is so different from that of the synoptics. On the one hand, John adopts the Hellenistic mythological pattern of the heavenly being who descends to earth in order to save men and then ascends again to heaven. He has Jesus himself say, "I have come down from heaven," (John 6:38) and, "I came from the Father and have come into the world; again, I am leaving the world and going to the Father." (John 16:28) When I say this is mythological, I do not mean it is untrue. Actually, the word "myth"——itself many-faceted——refers here to a way of speaking which goes beyond a factual account. Our deepest convictions are always myths, not facts. This mythological pattern of descending and ascending says in terms of space what incarnation says in more metaphysical terms.

On the other hand, John's Jesus preaches a different message from that in the synoptics. In John he constantly talks about himself, his origin, his mission in the world. In the synoptics Jesus seldom speaks about himself but about God's kingdom. All the Johannine "I am's"——such as "I am the door," "I am the bread of life," and "I am the light of the world"——are designed to let Jesus confront the world with his direct claim and so call for a decision for or against him.

The more we see how John presents Jesus, the more impossible it is for us to simply repeat what John says. There are three reasons for this. First, to speak today of a divine being who descended to earth would immediately make us think of an astronaut who parachuted to earth. That actually misses John's point, for an interplanetary astronaut still travels within the universe and does not enter it. Entry into the universe from a realm outside it is precisely what John asserts. But we cannot conceive of such a thing in a day when we regard the universe as constantly expanding and as consisting of countless galaxies. Therefore, simply to repeat John's Christology is to surrender its credibility.

Second, repeating it would also forfeit its meaning. In John's day, it was widely assumed that gods descended into the universe from the outside; therefore, John could talk this way about Jesus in order to raise the issue of whether or not Jesus himself came from God. In other words, because the descent-ascent pattern was widely taken for granted, John could use it to concentrate attention on Jesus. Just the opposite is true today. If we were to speak of Jesus in these terms, we would sidetrack the discussion to a debate over whether or not this way of thinking makes any sense and would probably never reach the point: whether Jesus is decisive or not. In John's day, the myth of the descent-ascent helped him make his point; today it stands in the way.

The third reason has to do with the content of the story of Jesus which John tells. Our historical understanding shows us that much of what John says about Jesus is not accurate history in the ordinary sense but, rather, is theological history. The sayings of Jesus in John are not the actual words of the historical Jesus, and almost no one is prepared to argue, or able to show, that they are. Moreover, because what the Johannine Jesus says and does is part and parcel of the overall view of Jesus, we cannot simply subtract the descent-ascent pattern and have the historical Jesus left. Consequently, whatever we do with John we must do with the whole gospel. It is, of course, true that John believes he is telling the truth about Jesus and the world; I believe it is also the case that, while what John says is not accurate history, it is profoundly true to historical experience.

What, then, are we to do with the penetrating and powerful portrait of Jesus? Do we merely admire this theology the way we admire an antique which we really would not want to own? That would sell John short and deprive ourselves as well. We owe it to John and to ourselves to look deeper. So we ask if what John says can be said in a fundamentally different way today. If so, then we could see whether or not this would agree with the historical Jesus. We shall, therefore, pursue this double assignment by dealing with three themes which make John distinctive in the New Testament.

An understanding of Jesus

We begin with John's assertion that the Son of God descended into the cosmos, down to the earth, where he became Jesus of Nazareth. Thus he is in the world but not of it. This makes Jesus the alien who identifies with us but who is not beholden to this world. As John's Jesus said during the

Last Supper, "The ruler of this world is coming; he has no power over me." (John 14:30) Jesus is the stranger who entered into the conditions of our lives in order to save us from them. We saw how John understood this. But even if we no longer think of the coming of the Son of God as the descent of an astronaut, can John's reason for saying this apply to the historical Jesus?

My suggestion is that the historical Jesus is as much an alien to our world as was the descended Son to John's. We recall that Albert Schweitzer concluded his survey of *The Quest of the Historical Jesus* by saying that "he comes to us as one unknown."[15] Schweitzer had discovered that Jesus was not the prototype of nineteenth-century liberal theology. Jesus was utterly different. He was a first-century Jew, not a nineteenth-century liberal Protestant ahead of the times.

Because Jesus is as alien to our world as he was to his, as much an intruder on our loyalties as was the Johannine Christ, and for reasons which are analogous, he confronted his age with the character of the age to come. Nineteen centuries have not succeeded in domesticating him completely. Time after time he stands over against us with the truth about ourselves. It is precisely his "otherness" that enables him to accost us. His consorting with sinners and Pharisees in order to make God's rule accessible to both, in terms which neither expects, confronts our assumption of where God's grace is at work just as it did theirs. The fact that he called both Simon the Zealot and Matthew, the Roman lackey, offends our propensity to establish an ideological community of either the establishment or the counter-establishment where all think alike because they are united by common hatreds. The Beatitudes announce that God's kingdom brings not only the consummation of all our values but also transvaluation.

We could go through the entire Jesus tradition to document this perception, but the point is clear enough already. This Jesus is so alien, so startling, so radically "other" that we can no more absorb him into our expectations than could the Samaritan woman. Jesus focuses the issues so that we either decide for him and break with the network of loyalties and assumptions which constitute our world, or, in the name of what we hold to be true, judge him to be an arrogant and erratic dreamer.

This is essentially what John's assertion that Jesus was God's Son who descended to earth attempts to account for. Such an assertion helps the reader understand why this man operates with such amazing and distressing authority (expressed in distinctively Johannine terms, of course), and why every encounter with him exposes alternatives that have ultimate consequences. It helps the reader to see that, faced with Jesus, most persons find it impossible to break out of their world and so put him out of it instead.

The debates of the Johannine Jesus and the Jews are designed to expose what is at issue between Jesus and the world as it is. Had John believed that the incarnation occurred in Greece, he would have reported similar debates with philosophers. Had John predicted the appearance of Jesus in America, he would have had to foresee analogous debates with us. We owe it to the synagogue today to make this clear. In other words, the proper way for us to interpret John's gospel is to enter into it, to extend the dynamic between Jesus and the Jews to ourselves. My point is that when the historical Jesus of the synoptics meets us, what transpires is what John reports: We are compelled to decide ultimate loyalties.

Our second theme is found at the end of John's prologue with the assertion that Jesus explains and interprets God; that is, he articulates him into the human situation so that God can be activated in the world which is originally and finally his. For John, Jesus can do this because he is the Word become flesh without ceasing to be God, or because he is the Son who was in the bosom of the Father before descending to earth. Moreover, the harsh and bitter debate in chapter 8 articulates God into the human situation in terms of the whence and whither of our obedience. When Jesus raises the question, "Who is your Father?", he asks about our whence and whither. To those who assert, "We have one Father, even God," Jesus responds, "If God were your Father you would love me. . .You are of your father the devil, and your will is to do your father's desires. . . . the reason why you do not hear them [the words of God which Jesus speaks] is that you are not of God." (John 8:39—47)

What is exposed here is the true issue in the understanding of God: Does that reality we call God merely function as a support mechanism for who we now are? Who God really is for us is determined by whose will we obey and to whom we consider ourselves accountable. In other words, the issue is whether or not the fundamental thing to be said about God turns out to be an ideology, a rationale for the status quo, which insulates us from the truth.

The historical Jesus does much the same thing when he articulates the kingdom of God into the human situation. By articulate I do not mean simply verbalizing, but making effective. It is useful here to recall Sidney Mead's insight that whatever else the term "God" means, it means that which is not man.[16] There is an irreducible otherness to God, an inescapable freedom to be God and to act as God with respect to the world as it is. Wherever this conception is impaired or obscured, God inevitably becomes the Ground of what is and the Consummator of what is already in process. The kingdom of God becomes the completion of our history and ceases to be the alternative to it.

But the kingdom of God which Jesus articulated transforms things. Fundamental to his perception of the kingdom is the apocalyptic theme of the great reversal: The last shall be first and the first, last. The Beatitudes are grounded in this motif. The situation of the downtrodden, the hungry, the weeping, the hated will be reversed, as will that of the rich, the sated, the rejoicing, the popular. (Luke 6:20–26) Jesus did not romanticize poverty, hunger, lamentation, and persecution. Though he did identify himself with the outcasts, it was not their social status in and of itself that gave them "squatters' rights" to the kingdom. Rather, Jesus pledges the kingdom to them because the plight of the poor and downtrodden is the symptom of a crooked world which is destined to be straightened out. Transforming the plight of the poor and the status of the rich is a particular instance of the rectification of all things. God's kingdom does not confirm the reward systems which now operate, but reconstitutes them because it makes all things right.

Further, when Jesus speaks of rewards, he is not talking about a payoff but is expressing the conviction that everything which already in this age is according to God's will shall be consummated. According to Matthew, those who are now merciful shall receive mercy then, and those who now make peace shall be called sons of God. This means that when all things are made straight, what is now aligned with God's will shall come into its own, find its reward. In short, God's kingdom is reversal and corroboration, judgment and salvation. But if this is the case, then Jesus realigns our understanding of who God is and what it means for him to be king. And when Jesus realigns our understanding of God, it is impossible to turn him into the ultimate sanction of the values of the status quo.

Jesus articulates this rectifying God into the human situation in such a way that God can no longer be reduced to an idea that must be clarified or to the ultimate sanction for what we already are and trust. Instead, God now means the Righteous Power who surprises us with both his gift and demand. When Jesus concentrates religion on the uncompromised love for God and for neighbor, he sets before us a demand which cannot be surpassed, while at the same time gifting us with a clarification of what life is all about. When he seems to be uninterested in meeting his family, saying of the crowd around him, "Here are my mother and my brothers, for whoever does the will of my Father in heaven is my brother, and my sister and mother," he locates that demand which gives us our true family and so rebuilds our loyalties. When he tells of the pearl merchant who found the ultimate pearl, he tells us that God's kingdom is the surprising good fortune which demands a total wager of the self.

In all such ways, Jesus shows us that the problem of God is not that of a difficult idea to master but of a difficult loyalty; the real issue is God or mammon because where the heart is, there is the treasure. When he rebukes Peter for tempting him with messianic power, he surprises us with the assertion that God's rule comes by suffering. Likewise, Jesus asserts that our trust in God manifests itself in leaving the reward for piety to the One who sees in secret.

At every point, this God-obsessed man articulates the God of the New Age into the present in such a way as to reconstitute our relation to God. To those who are grasped by his word and work, God becomes Father. When Jesus reveals, or unconceals, God, he does not tell us new information about him but reconstitutes our relation to him. Because he identified himself so fully with the will of God, the contours of his life constitute a parable of God, a narrative which opens up for us who God truly is. In short, the historical Jesus, like the Johannine, explains what the reality, God, actually means and requires of us. He does so by setting us in such a relation to him that whenever we get lost or bewildered, we thread our way back to Jesus in whose presence we find ourselves rightly related to God afresh. Here, too, the historical Jesus really does what John says the Son from the Father's bosom does.

The "now" of salvation

This brings us to the third consideration——John's emphasis on the "now" of salvation. As we have seen, the strength of the Pauline insistence on the "not yet" of salvation is that it guards against all enthusiastic claims for every present. The Spirit is the down payment, not the full payment; it is the experienced pledge, not the fulfilled promise. But for John, salvation is truly present, not merely begun, when men respond rightly to Jesus. For John, whoever believes in Jesus has made the ultimate decision and so enters into life that is eternal. Eternal life is not sheer perpetuity; more of the same is not eternity. Eternal life is a quality of life which is impervious to deadness of soul. As Jesus told Martha, "Whoever lives and believes in me shall never die." (John 11:26) This is the Johannine restatement and correction of the traditional view formulated in the preceding sentence: "He who believes in me, though he die, yet shall he live." John accepts this traditional view which points to future resurrection, but he immediately corrects it by saying that eternal life is now.

Moreover, in the farewell discourses at the Last Supper (John 13—17), Jesus speaks of the disciples remaining in him even though he is about to depart from them. How can one abide in Jesus when he is gone? The answer is by abiding in his love, which is immediately interpreted as keeping his commandments. In other words, love is the modality of life which is impervious to death; for death separates but love unites. Just as death separates us from one another and from God, so love unites us to one another and to God. The ultimate criterion for love is willingness to surrender to death for the sake of another. "Greater love has no man than this, that a man lay down his life for his friend." (John 15:13)

Furthermore, where love lives, there the Father and the Son are found. "If a man loves me he will keep my word and my Father will love him, and we will come to him and make our home with him." (John 14:23) Thus John relativizes the difference between heaven and earth, then and now; for if the Father and the Son come to live with the believer in history, then there is virtually no difference between life now and life after death when the believer moves to the Father's house (John 14:1ff.). Either way, the Father and the Son are with the sons of God, insofar as their existence is shaped by love.

Is this only a Johannine theory, or is it groundable in the Jesus of history? This is an exceedingly difficult question to answer clearly and convincingly. The evidence is complex and the issues are subtle, partly because they involve the understanding of fundamental categories such as time and futurity. Nonetheless, the question is important and deserves as clear an answer as possible.

Three things need to be said in any case. First, even though John emphasizes the nowness of salvation, he does not eliminate the future altogether. There are occasional references to the future resurrection. Whether these are later additions to the text, as Bultmann thought, or the evangelist himself being careful to acknowledge the traditional view, the result is that the fourth gospel does see something of salvation beyond the present. (The same point is implied in the fact that while the believers are in the world now, after death they shall also be taken from it.) Something of the futurity of salvation remains even in John.

Second, though the historical Jesus was oriented to the future, he did not merely prepare men for what was to come. Herein lies one of the fundamental differences between Jesus and John the Baptist: John the Baptist prepared men for the future, the character of which they did not begin to enjoy ahead of time; Jesus began celebrating the kingdom now. This is why Jesus said John played funeral but he himself played wedding. This is why Jesus could be called a convivial wine-bibber, for many of his meals were anticipations of the messianic banquet.

The third thing to be said, therefore, is that in comparing the historical Jesus with the Johannine Jesus, we are faced with a difference in balance, not with absolute contrast. Present as well as future salvation are to be found in both, but in different proportions. John has accentuated to the full the nowness of salvation which is actually implied in Jesus' own work.

The question then is two-fold: Does the historical Jesus break open salvation for us now, and, if so, what are its contours? Our answer has already been given in a way which agrees with John. If Jesus restructures our relation to the God whose will he embodies, then we are saved from allegiance to that which is not God. In fact, like the Jews in the fourth gospel, we are not aware that the god who is operational in our lives is not God until Jesus exposes our idolatry. Idolatry may seem a strange word to use of an age that likes to think it is secular. The real question, however, is not whether or not our time can believe in God, but whether or not that which we finally trust is trustworthy, whether or not our trusting it confers life and releases love and compassion. The more aware we are of the tyranny of bitterness, of sheer contempt and hatred for others, the more evident it is that our deepest trust does not release love but death. If in this situation trusting Jesus and thereby trusting the God who shaped him to be what he was frees us to love, we are indeed saved from the deadness that erodes our souls. Love is precisely what breaks us loose from the bondage to this world.

The Flesh becomes word

Finally, we are in a position to speak of the ways in which the Flesh becomes word. In this context, "Flesh" is a way of speaking of the historical Jesus, the Jesus who is discerned through critical analysis of the synoptics. But how does he become word? I do not mean to suggest that there is some alchemy by which this historical figure is transmuted into the Johannine Logos. Rather, what the phrase "the Flesh becomes word" signals is a different understanding of the term "word," namely as "message." Furthermore, the phrase deliberately uses the present tense of the verb and not the past, because the point is not that the historical Jesus once became a word but that he becomes word ever anew. Our question, then, is how this figure of the past becomes a message in our day.

It is well known that Bultmann insisted that the gospel is the Word of God and that it is illegitimate to make the Word of God into a piece of history, because history is ambiguous and a matter of probability. Therefore, Bultmann also insisted that the historical Jesus is not the gospel even if we knew his history completely and accurately. In my book, *A Future for the Historical Jesus*, I argued against this position and suggested how the historical Jesus, the Jesus whom the critical historian reconstructs from the gospels, can function in preaching and theology. I shall not summarize that discussion but shall draw on it as I relate my reflections explicitly to the theme of the fourth gospel.

We have been reflecting on the key line in the prologue which begins "the Word became flesh"; now I want to turn to the concluding line which says "we have seen his glory." What is this glory? John provides the clue when he concludes the story of the wedding at Cana by commenting, "This, the first of his signs, Jesus did at Cana in Galilee and manifested his glory; and his disciples believed in him." (John 2:11) That is, the glory of Jesus is exposed in the miracles when these are understood as signs. If they are not seen as signs, they remain nothing more than miracles. This concept is underscored in Chapter 6, where the crowds follow Jesus after the great feeding. He says to them, "You seek me not because you saw signs but because you ate your fill of the loaves." (John 6:26)

What makes a miracle into a sign? For John, it is seeing in the event a deeper meaning, seeing an aperture into the saving significance of what Jesus did. In the Cana story, the fact that Jesus turned 240 gallons of purification water into the best wine at a party is more than a stupendous feat; it is a sign of his ability to transform the water of religion into the life-giving wine. Whether one sees only the miracle or sees also the sign depends on whether or not one drinks the wine and is thereby transformed. This is why John says that the disciples believed in Jesus.

Now we understand why John's prologue says "we have seen his glory." The only way to speak of his glory is as a confession of what we have seen in him. In John, most of the spectators look only at the event and do not see into it as the pointer to the meaning of Jesus. For this reason John repeatedly shows that the greater the miracle, the greater the offense. John even reports that once a voice from heaven spoke to Jesus in public, but the crowd thought it thundered (John 12:27—30). What John concentrates on the miracles, he implies for the whole gospel——that is, the whole event of Jesus is a signpost to his real meaning, a meaning which can be spoken of only as a confession, "This is what we have seen in him."

In keeping with the Johannine perspective, I suggest that today the Flesh becomes word when we are grasped by the event of Jesus in such a way that we can bear witness to what we have seen in him, the historical Jesus. For evangelism, this is decisive. The day is past when we can simply sketch the life of Jesus, or parts of it, and assume that the hearers will understand it to be the work of God for them. In our post—Christian era, people can hear a report of the historical Jesus, be it ever so accurate and grounded in critical analysis of the sources, and still say, "O.K., so he said this or did that. So what?" The Jesus who is reconstructed from the gospels is ambiguous because he is historical, for no piece of history interprets and validates itself. At the same time, this piece of history called Jesus has broken open for us the true meaning of God, has conferred on us a quality of life which will not let us go. This is why we can say with John, "we have seen his glory." Without this confession, the Flesh remains flesh, the historical Jesus remains a historical figure, and no word arises. But with our own testimony, he becomes a word to our time.

Let me summarize. First, the Christian gospel centers in the meaning of Jesus for man's relation to God and to his fellows. Second, we cannot talk about the meaning of Jesus without talking about Jesus himself. Third, nowadays we cannot simply repeat the story of Jesus the way John tells it, because we know that, though it may be true, it is not accurate history in the ordinary sense. Fourth, John's gospel nonetheless does suggest one way in which we can preach the historical Jesus whom we reach by historical analysis of the synoptics. This suggestion is that we are to bear witness to the way in which the historical Jesus cuts across our lives and heals our relation to God and man. When we do that we are in line with John who said, "we have seen his glory," even if we are not speaking of the glory of the pre-existent Son who came down from the bosom of the Father. An objective account of Jesus himself is very important, but it is only a piece of news; it becomes a piece of *good* news when the reporter testifies that through this event he himself has been liberated. Fifth, the words to Nicodemus apply to us: "We speak of what we know, and bear witness to what we have seen." (John 3:11) On the surface, these words reassure us that we know what we are talking about. Under the surface, however, they rob us of our security because they remind us that our word is tethered to what we have come to know for ourselves.

So the question before us is this: In seeing the historical Jesus, have you seen any glory? If you have, you have a gospel. And when you have this gospel, the Flesh becomes word again. And when this Flesh becomes word, life comes into death, freedom into bondage. When that happens, we shall have found the power to become the sons of God in the here and now. Then we can be true evangelists.

NOTES

1. Basic articles which debate these questions are found in *Apocalypticism, Journal for Theology and the Church*, vol. 6 (New York: Herder & Herder, 1969).

2. See Jürgen Moltmann, *Theology of Hope*, trans. J. W. Leitch (New York: Harper & Row, 1969); Wolfhart Pannenberg et al. *Revelation as History*, trans. David Grauskou (New York: Macmillan, 1968); Wolfhart Pannenberg, *Theology and the Kingdom of God* (Philadelphia: Fortress Press, 1969).

3. Carl E. Braaten, *Christ and Counter-Christ: Apocalyptic Themes in Theology and Culture* (Philadelphia: Fortress Press, 1972).

4. A vigorous theological statement reflecting the Third World is Rubem Alves's *A Theology of Human Hope* (New York/ Cleveland: Corpus Books, 1969). For an impassioned discussion reflecting the bitter African experience, see Colin Morris, *Include Me Out!* (London: Epworth Press, 1968).

5. Philadelphia: Westminster, 1969.

6. The most recent, thorough survey of apocalyptic is that by D. S. Russell, *The Method and Message of Jewish Apocalyptic* (Philadelphia: Westminster, 1964). For a sketch, see Leon Morris, *Apocalyptic* (Grand Rapids: Eerdmans, 1972).

7. Eugen Rosenstock-Huessy put it well: "That which simply goes on from the past as a trend is not 'future' in the full sense of the term. It simply travels on an extension visa from the past.... The relation of any past and any future is never made by a trend, but always by a victory over trends." *The Christian Future* (New York: Harper & Row, Harper Torchbook, 1966), p. 32.

8. For a survey of New Testament ideas of death and resurrection and their relation to contemporary Hellenistic motifs, see my contribution, "New Testament Views of Death," in *Perspectives on Death*, ed. Liston O. Mills (Nashville: Abingdon, 1969), pp. 33-98.

9. Jacques Ellul, *The Presence of the Kingdom*, trans. Olive Wyon (New York: Seabury, 1967), pp. 74ff. From a non-Christian perspective, a similar point is made by Herbert Marcuse, *One-Dimensional Man* (Boston: Beacon, 1964).

10. J. L. Talmon, *The Origins of Totalitarian Democracy* (London: Sphere Books, Ltd., 1970).

11. "Harlem, Rebellion and Resurrection," in *Theological Crossings*, ed. Alan Geyer and Dean Peerman (Grand Rapids: Eerdmans, 1969), p. 131.

12. This is the burden of Jacques Ellul's *False Presence of the Kingdom,* trans. C. E. Hopkin (New York: Seabury, 1972).

13. J. Louis Martyn, *History and Theology in the Fourth Gospel* (New York: Harper and Row, 1968).

14. In his provocative book on John, Ernst Kasemann formulated it as follows: For John, "faith means one thing only: to know who Jesus is." *The Testament of Jesus,* trans. Gerhard Krodel (Philadelphia: Fortress Press, 1968), p. 25.

15. Albert Schweitzer, *The Quest of the Historical Jesus* (London: A. & C. Black, 1952), p. 401.

16. "In Quest of America's Religion," in *Theological Crossings,* ed. Alan Geyer and Dean Peerman (Grand Rapids: Eerdmans, 1969), p. 94. Equally trenchant is Eugen Rosenstock-Huessy's comment that "we know God primarily because we know that we are not gods but would like to be." *The Christian Future* (New York: Harper & Row, Harper Torchbook, 1966), p.96.

CHAPTER 4

AN EVANGELISM ADEQUATE FOR TODAY

by the Reverend Leighton Ford

The Reverend Leighton Ford has been with the Billy Graham Association since 1955 and is now Vice-President. He alternates with Mr. Graham on the radio program "Hour of Decision"; his own daily TV program, "Insight," is featured in a number of cities. He is a graduate of Wheaton College and Columbia Theological Seminary.

4

I would like to draw your attention to the twentieth chapter of John's gospel, the scene where Jesus came to the disciples after the crucifixion. That evening the disciples were meeting behind locked doors in fear of the Jewish leaders, when suddenly Jesus was standing there among them. After greeting them and saying "Peace," he showed them his hands and his side. How wonderful was their joy as they saw their Lord! He spoke to them again and said, "As the Father has sent me, even so I am sending you." Then he breathed on them and told them, "Receive the Holy Spirit. If you forgive anyone's sins, they are forgiven. If you refuse to forgive them, they are unforgiven."

Kenneth Scott Latourette, certainly outstanding among all the contemporary historians of the Christian church, once said that the surge of the movement of the Spirit of God across the face of the earth was very much like the tides of the sea. There comes a period of ebb and a period of flow, a period when the tides are high on the beach and then they retreat. But in retreat, the tides seem to gather momentum, and when they move in again it is to a higher spot on the beach. In the past decade I think we have seen the ebb. We have seen periods of despair, disillusionment, and discouragement within the church. Now I think we are beginning to see the tide move in on the beach again. I believe today is a great day to be called by God to be a herald of Jesus Christ.

The signs are multiplying. Take the movement of the Holy

Spirit among young people, for example. Who would have thought a decade ago there would ever come a time when Jesus was more popular than the Beatles? New lay movements—lay renewal, great evangelistic movements in many parts of the world—are setting a record of church growth. A decade ago everybody was talking in despair about the dwindling of Christian forces around the globe. Now researchers such as David Barrett of Nairobi say that if the trend continues, by the end of the century the world's population will have its greatest proportion of Christians in the history of Christianity.

We are beginning to heal the pietist-activist breach that has stymied us for so long. For several generations at least, we have behaved in the church very much according to an old statute that I understand is still on the books in Massachusetts: "If two vehicles come to the crossroads at the same time, both shall stop and neither shall move until the other has passed." Are we to be soul winners or social reformers? The healing over of this split is another of the many signs that the tide is moving in again upon the beach.

We certainly have witnessed the responsiveness in the work of evangelism to which God has called us. But in this day of new opportunities, with a new wind blowing and a new tide flowing, the church has often been boxed in, unable to penetrate the world with real power. We have found ourselves in a "holy huddle" like a football team deep in its own end zone late in the game, unable to move the ball. On the field are twenty-two men who need rest, and in the stands are 50,000 who need exercise. Those on the field appear to spend most of their time in the huddle. Sometimes it seems we have forgotten the plays and even the purpose of the game. Perhaps we like the security; I have never heard of anybody getting hurt in the huddle. We seem to like to stay there and discuss and analyze our strategy, view the enemy, and criticize each other, but the result is that we remain boxed in.

We find ourselves in a situation similar to that of those disciples of our Lord, huddled together in that little upper room behind locked doors. Then our Lord walked into that room and said three things. He gave a greeting: "Peace be with you." He issued a command: "As my Father sent me, so I send you into this world." He offered a promise, breathing on them in an acted-out parable and saying: "Receive the Holy Spirit." These words of our Lord were the keys that opened the door and thrust that little timid, whipped, beaten group of men out into the world. Within a quarter of a century they carried out a revolution.

It seems to me our Lord is handing us the same keys today. There are many games we Christians play, however, and I think we are now playing "Key, key, who's got the key?" I am not talking about Key 73, though it may be apropos.

There seem to be three different groups within the church, each pushing and shoving, trying to get to the door and saying, "We've got the key. Just let *us* get at the door. We've got the key to an effective witness for the church!"

One group says the key is *proclamation*. Just preach the simple gospel of Christ; it's the power of God to salvation. Another group says the key is *presence*——Christian presence in the world. We're to be salt; we're to be light; we're to be involved in the world. Just be there. That's the key to witness: presence. Then there is a third group, especially active in the last four or five years, which says, in effect, the key is *power*. "You shall receive power after the Holy Spirit has come upon you. We need to open ourselves to the Holy Spirit and as he moves into our lives, takes us and uses us, we will be able to have an effective ministry. We've got the key."

The irony is that the lock on the door is a triple lock. One key will not open it. It takes three keys to turn the lock and open the door. I believe that our Lord, in his grace and his sovereignty, is saying to the church in our day, "Take these keys, all of them, and use them."

The key of proclamation

Take the key of proclamation, a bold proclamation of the apostolic gospel in all of its truth. Proclaim it!

Our Lord came into that room to a group of spiritual cop-outs and said, "Peace be with you." He showed them his hands to say, "Do you see those nail prints?" He showed them his side to say, "Do you see where the spear went?" He was not offering them some vague, mythical, mystical peace hung on nothing. He was offering them peace based on what he had done in time, space, and history by his death and resurrection. By his death he offered peace of conscience and forgiveness for their guilt. By his resurrection he offered peace of mind, establishing himself in his risen power as Lord and Messiah.

One of the things we need desperately today in the work of evangelism is to recover that sense of truth in the gospel. We don't have a vague message to preach. Rabbi Duncan, who taught Hebrew at New College, Edinburgh, remarked about a popular preacher of his day, saying that he "preached the gospel or something or other about a Jesus or someone or other who died on a cross or something or other for our sins or something or other." We have been given a message with content to it! We preach, as the song says, "Christ crucified and Christ risen." Paul said, "I deliver unto you all that which I first received, that Christ died for our sins according to the scripture, that he was buried, and that he arose again the third day according to the scripture."

A. M. Hunter, the British theologian, has suggested that if a reporter had gone to a meeting of the early church and taken notes, he would have come out with a very concrete understanding of what the people believed, what they were saying, and what it meant to be a Christian. He would have heard them say that Jesus came, went about doing good, was crucified, rose again, ascended, and sent the Holy Spirit. Men were to break from their old way of life in repentance and turn to God in a new way of life through faith. The gift of the Holy Spirit would be given to them, and they would be baptized in the name of Christ. The reporter would know what they had said. I sometimes wonder what the reporter would do if he heard our message today. It was said the disciples were glad when they saw the Lord. I think you would have to say that the disciples are confused today, not knowing what is this gospel, this message, and wondering if there is anything to it.

It is difficult today to maintain the definite historic content of the gospel. It is difficult because of the "now" bias of our age: The only thing that is relevant is the new. It is difficult because of the craze for sensation, for emotion. Now I'm for emotion. I happen to be a Presbyterian, and our chief problem has not been emotionalism. I can understand this desire to feel that we have a problem today in the church because we have been so sterile. I think we can understand the antirational kick that many young people are on: They have seen a human reason which puts men on the moon and pollution in our rivers. They say, "If that's reason, I don't want any part of it," and they look for a different level of mystical experience. Drugs, in many instances, afford that leap into ecstasy where the mind is disregarded.

I talked with a young man in Charlotte recently whose mind was blown on drugs. He had come out to my mother-in-law's home on a Sunday afternoon. She's an elderly lady, living alone, and she was afraid. She called the police and the young man was picked up. I made an appointment to talk with him.

"You know, they didn't put me in jail," he said. "That wasn't a jail; that was a church." He wasn't saying that jail was a church simply because God was there. He was saying it was a church because there was absolutely no distinction in his mind. He had one of those experiences when everything melts together without discrimination: No longer is there yes and no, truth and error. I believe that it is tremendously important in our day to preach the gospel with a sense of what Francis Schaeffer calls "true truth." And, in our day, that is difficult.

Someone has said that when men stop believing in God, they don't believe in nothing; they believe in anything. In one sense that makes it easier to preach the gospel today than ever before. But it makes it more difficult to preach the gospel intelligibly and with some distinction as to what the gospel means. That is why I think we must have a tough-mindedness in matters of belief if we are to speak the gospel to twentieth-century man.

Jesus is not just a trip. Jesus is not just another psychedelic experience. There is a truth content based in history that can be declared, defined, and, I believe, verified. This truth is to be the basis of the message we proclaim: He showed them his hands and his side. One young person said, "If you Christians can't stick to that truth, then spike your communion wine with LSD and take a trip with the rest of us."

I am all for what's happening in many aspects of the Jesus Movement. I think we need their verve, their excitement, their enthusiasm, their innovations in our church. But one thing that concerns me—not only in the "hippie" Jesus Movement, but in many of the movements among young people today—is a failure to understand the place of the mind. God says, "Be ye not as the horse or the mule which has no understanding." We are to love the Lord our God with all our minds. Jesus taught; he came as a teacher. Paul described conversion as obeying the truth. Evangelism today must declare that truth content of the gospel and declare it in a way that is clear. Then people can understand what they need to believe and do to be Christians.

I remember driving to the airport in Seattle one day. A friend was taking me, and we spent thirty minutes trying to get on a new expressway. There were no access signs showing the way. It was one of the most frustrating experiences I have ever had—seeing the cars whizzing by, knowing we should be at the airport in twenty minutes, and not being able to figure out how to get on the thing. Many times we have said to people, "Here's the Christian style of life; here's the new life Christ offers." And they say, "How do I get on the thing?"

Can you state it clearly so that someone else can understand? "This is what it means to be a Christian. This is how I respond, how I receive Jesus Christ." Is all of this coming through in our preaching of the gospel?

I have been reading Dr. George Peter's analysis of "New Life for All." Nigeria was the site of this drive, one of the great evangelistic saturation movements of our day, one of the great stories of the last several years. Dr. Peter says that one of the strongest notes of "New Life for All" is the message putting the gospel in simple terms: "God has given life to all men. Life has been forfeited by all men because of sin. God has offered new life to us through Jesus Christ, and we can receive that through faith and repentance. Then we're to express that light in every relationship of life." Tens of thousands of Christians in Nigeria took this simple five-point outline, learned it, began to understand what it meant, and shared it with the entire country. Dr. Peter said that the force of seeing that message stated again and again and again moved the soul of the nation.

Now I know it is easy to become stereotyped, to become caricatured, to have one narrow way, and to say everyone must respond to Christ in just one way. That is a danger. But Jesus did not heal every blind man the same way. He put mud on the eyes of one person. To another he said, "Be healed." Wouldn't it have been ridiculous if later one of these men had asked the other, "What did Jesus do for you?" The answer might have been, "Well, he gave me my sight back."

"Oh, did he put mud on your eyes?"

"No. He just said, 'Receive it.' "

"You mean he didn't put mud packs on your eyes? Why man, you're still blind! You've got to have mud on your eyes."

If those ex-blind men had been like us, two different denominations would have immediately been formed: the mudites and the anti-mudites. No one comes to Christ with the same words or the same verbal formula or the same experience. There is no *one* way to experience Christ.

Just as dangerous, however, is having *no* way. It is very easy to titter and smirk when we hear of things like Campus Crusade for Christ's four spiritual laws. But they have been able to reach many people with a formula which says simply, "Look, God loves you. He has a plan for your life. We've been separated from God because of our sin. God has made a provision, a bridge through Jesus Christ by which we can come back to him. You can receive him by a personal invitation."

I might state this formula differently perhaps, but we need to have some way, true to our own integrity, to state with clarity: "This is what the gospel means, and this is how you respond." Then we must proclaim our message with expectancy.

Have we lost that sense of expectancy? This message is dynamite! When we preach Jesus Christ, we proclaim release. This is the biblical understanding of preaching. New Testament preaching is not just talking about an event that happened in the past. New Testament preaching is declaring the present event of Jesus Christ. As we proclaim this event, the Holy Spirit takes this proclamation and applies it. Then, freedom and release happen in the lives of people; we have seen it happen again and again.

I think of a young fellow in California whose name is Rick Careno, number two leader in the Hell's Angels. Once when he was strung out on an overdose of drugs, his buddies dropped him in one of those big trash containers in a back alley in Los Angeles. They left him there to die. Rick lay there four days and four nights in his filth, his sickness, and his vomit. Somehow after four days he got the strength to pull himself out. Dragging himself home, he told his mother, "I'm going to die unless I get some help."

"Why don't you go to Angel Stadium," she said, "where Billy Graham is preaching?"

He said, "Mama, I don't need religion."

"He's not talking about religion," she explained. "He's talking about a person, about Jesus Christ."

Rick Careno went to the stadium. The first two nights his mind was so blown he did not understand a word that was said. He was in such despair that he even tried to walk in front of a train but failed.

The fourth night he thought, "I've just got to get down there in the stadium and talk to that man." He ran out onto the turf wearing his Hell's Angels jacket. He hadn't had a bath in eight months, literally. The security men saw him and thought he was trying to attack someone, so they stopped him. One of the Graham team members sat down and talked with him about the reality of the person of Jesus Christ in whom God had stepped into history. Enough penetrated Rick's mind that he began to understand, and he came back. You could see the change in his life—like a series of lapsed-time photos of a flower unfolding.

Five nights later he brought his mother up to the platform and introduced her to some members of the team. He put his arm around her and said, "This is my mama." She stood there with tears streaming down her face and said, "This is the first time in years I can remember Rick touching me and saying he loved me."

I remember another man, named Jim, who was the ring-leader in the racial difficulty in his city. I talked to him one time about the things he said when he addressed a crowd. "I know how to incite a crowd," he explained. "I know the code words I can use. I know how I can get the feelings going because I've been a strikebreaker. The governor of my state had me working for him. But on a trip to New York City, I went to Madison Square Garden, and I heard Billy Graham preaching the gospel of Jesus Christ. I couldn't really believe that God would want me. Then a Christian pastor in my city came to my store at my daughter's request and talked to me about Jesus Christ. I received him into my life."

"Jim," I asked, "did you believe those things you used to say, those racial slurs and all?"

He replied, "Yes, I did. You see, I had to be better than somebody. But once I came to know the love of God in Jesus Christ, I no longer had to prove myself better than anybody."

The dynamics of conversion changed that man. There is power in this gospel we proclaim. Take the key of proclamation, says our Lord.

The key of presence

I believe that proclamation involves not simply what we say, but how we say it: communication. Jesus is not only the content of our message; Jesus is also the pattern of our proclamation. "As my Father sent me," he said, "so I send you." When God our Father wanted to communicate his message of liberation, love, and new life, how did he do it? He didn't send a tape recording; he didn't shout down the message. He came. The Word became flesh and dwelt among us. He visited and redeemed his people by being born in this world, living in this world, and overcoming sin on that cross. It was complete identification, for he came among us; and when he spoke, they listened. The impact was not just in what he said about the kingdom. It was how he did it. The king had come as a servant to live among men.

It seems to me that here we have the key of incarnation, of genuine Christian presence——the Holy Spirit in the church, the extension of the incarnation. If our message is going to be heard, it must be heard in our day as it was through our Lord: through those who are willing to become one, those who are willing to identify with others as he identified. This is the hardest part for me, not only to speak but really to feel, to touch, to listen, to act, and to reach out as Jesus did. This is not so easy.

As Christ was in the world, so are we. But what was he in the world? He was not simply here; he was here as God's model, the model of who God is and the model of what God intended genuine humanity to be. Jesus said, "He that has seen me has seen the Father." He was the model of the reality of God.

I believe God has put the church here as his model. Tom Skinner has a tremendous message on God's new community. This community is composed of a different kind of people— a "third race," as the early church was called. This community not only speaks peace but embodies in its very being the peace, love, justice, and reconciliation which Christ came to bring. As I understand salvation, it means a healing of all the broken relationships in which man's fall has involved us. When you go back to the beginning, back to the Garden, as Joni Mitchell sang in "Woodstock," you see man alienated from God, the beginning of spiritual alienation. Then what happens? Psychological alienation sets in. Something dies within man. Cain kills Abel—the sociological alienation. That is where hatred, war, and conflict begin. The ground is cursed as man falls, and ecological alienation divides man from God, from himself, from his brothers and neighbors, and from the world in which he lives.

I believe that the salvation of God includes the healing of all of these broken relationships, beginning with the justification of our relationship to him. "Being justified by faith, we have peace with God through our Lord Jesus Christ." (Romans 5:1) He died to bring us that peace. Then as our restored relationship with God changes us and transforms us, it brings about the healing of the other broken areas of our lives. God does not grant a perfect healing—though that will come—but there ought to be evident in the body of Christ a substantial healing of brokenness. Our words of peace will be dead words unless they are spoken from the demonstration of the reality of peace in Christ's people. We hardly dare to utter the word, lest we be like the Old Testament prophets who said there was peace when there was no peace.

I remember preaching one Sunday morning in a beautiful church on the story of Zacchaeus and Jesus, who came to seek and save the lost. After the service somebody told me that a young serviceman on his way to Vietnam had come that morning to hear me preach, but he had been denied admission because he was black. The people at the door called him a demonstrator. I found out who he was, and I got his address. I wrote to him, and I told him how ashamed I was, that I didn't know until later what had happened. When one of my friends went to Vietnam, I asked him to visit this young man, and they had a wonderful conversation about the Lord.

I had made it quite plain that I would not speak in the name of Christ anywhere anyone was to be denied. I couldn't help asking myself what message had been heard that day. Was it that Jesus came to seek and save the lost? Or was it that he came to seek and save the *white* lost? What did the *word* mean without the *presence*?

In contrast to this occasion was a series of three meetings held at the University of Virginia. The students wanted to call the series "Jesus Christ versus Christianity." That really bugged me at first, but one day I got to thinking about the first three chapters of the book of Revelation. I read through them, and five times Jesus says, "I am against Christianity; I have something against you." So we had those meetings.

Three of us made up the team: Black evangelist Tom Skinner, a long-haired folk singer from California, and me— the WASP in the middle, I guess. Jesus, however, broke through the stereotypes, the caricatures. And God moved through the narrow middle-class preconceptions of some of those students.

On the last night I remained to talk to a few people. A young man came and sat near me. After everyone else had gone, this long-haired, gentle-looking man said, "Mr. Ford, do you remember Friday night?" I had asked the students that Friday to do a survey by filling out a form—"When I think of Christianity I think of. . . ." I had picked the four most vitriolic responses to read the first night.

"Do you remember those statements you read?" the man asked. "Do you remember the first one?"

"Yes," I answered.

"When I think of Christianity," the first one had declared, "I think of colonialism, nationalism, rights of primacy, the Thirty Years' War. . . ." The accusations went on and on.

"I wrote that," he said. Then he smiled and added, "I became a Christian Friday night."

I think this outcome resulted partly because a presence was embodied there, a presence which crossed cultural distinctions. Jesus Christ was there. I believe that kind of presence means many things. It means going to people where they are. As a British Evangelical Alliance report said, "Evangelism ought to be of the church but it ought not always to be in it." Evangelism means going where the people are, as our Lord Jesus did.

Alan Walker has done this for years in Australia, taking me for services on Sunday night to a theater instead of the sanctuary of a church, going where the people are used to going. Why don't we do this? Why don't we have our Christmas and Easter concerts in a shopping mall sometime instead of a church? That is, if the choir is good enough. Instead of paying to put our Sunday morning broadcast on the air, why not take that same amount of money and put a short message about Christ in a commercial spot during a football game on Friday night or Saturday afternoon? Let's learn to think of going where the people are.

I believe that this kind of presence also means concern for people as they are: people whose emotions have been rubbed so raw that they can hardly hear the words we say, young people who are convinced that Jesus is the pillar of the power structure, black people who are convinced that he is Whitey's God.

Kids who have been brought up in the ghetto have no idea what a "Father in Heaven" means. Carl Burke told about an ex-convict who translated "the Lord is my Shepherd" as "the Lord is my Parole Officer." A parole officer had been like a father to him, so that was his image of God. To reach people like this, our words have to be fleshed out in genuine concern for love and justice. I believe that God is moving in that way. Among evangelical Christians—and I am thankful to be one—a new wind is blowing. A new time is upon us.

We saw this during the Congress on Evangelism in Minneapolis several years ago when speaker after speaker smashed the stereotype of evangelism as a narrow little pious thing. One of the speakers said, "You know, we've been like the old steamboat. When it whistled it couldn't move, and when it moved it couldn't whistle." Let's learn to whistle *and* move. Let's learn to speak the word and act the word in the needs where people find themselves.

In various ways we have tried to do this in some of my own Reach Out crusades. In Rochester, New York, for example, our Christian Action Committee said, "Let's pick something in this area where we can give, not only in word but in deed, a demonstration of concern in the name of Christ." As a result of that Reach Out we established a program called "Bridge" in Attica Prison, thirty miles from Rochester. Volunteers from the churches in Rochester and Buffalo go to Attica every week visiting certain prisoners there, befriending them, and helping them to get established on their release. In this way Christians are giving some deep indication in deed, in presence, of the love of Christ.

The key of power

The third key is the key of power. Jesus breathed on a group of whipped, defeated men living with the memory of their failure and also with the prospect of persecution by their enemies on the outside. Jesus said, "Receive the Holy Spirit," and these men became transformed. I believe that God is breathing on us today. Of this charismatic renewal President John McKay of Princeton has said, "I believe that this is the chief hope of the ecumenical tomorrow." Bishop Leslie Newcomb of India said that if we want to ask where the church is, we must ask not only where the message is and where the structure is, but also where the Holy Spirit is visibly present in power.

In this day when we have heard that God is dead, our Lord has stretched forth his hand with a kind of wry irony and said, "Dead, am I?" And he has breathed upon his church again with new power.

One of the greatest mistakes we have ever made is to allow the charismatic movement to be called the "charismatic movement." If you are part of the church, you are part of the charismatic movement. The charismatic movement is the body of Christ. The charismatic movement is the church with different gifts: wisdom, proclamation, knowledge, the prophetic voice. Given here is the gift of healing and there, perhaps, the gift of tongues. But all gifts are for the body of which we are all part. If we are not part of the charismatic movement, then we are outside the stream of what Jesus Christ our Lord is doing.

We are beginning to see today, in a new way, that the Spirit of Jesus is the same Spirit who moved upon the void at the beginning. He is the Spirit of Creation. He is the Spirit of Liberation, of Salvation. "The Spirit of the Lord is upon me. He has anointed me to proclaim relief to the captives." And the Spirit of Creation and the Spirit of Salvation are moving together. We are beginning to say today that unless our experience of the Holy Spirit is translated into action in this world in which we live, it is not valid. Unless our work in this world of social concern is based on the impetus of the renewing power of the Holy Spirit, it is empty. A new thing is happening.

Perhaps one of the saddest marks of those of us in the church in North America has been our spiritual weakness and anemia, our prayerlessness. We have felt we could do it on our own. As a friend of mine said, "We have had all the power we needed——for the job we were doing." If only God would breathe on us again, we could see our world in its hunger and its brokenness, its conflict and its loneliness. We could see ourselves as we are and our Lord as he is. We must kneel and say again, "Blow! Wind of God, blow!"

The first night of the Billy Graham crusade in New York City in 1956, somebody came to me and said, "Quick! Come! A clergyman has come forward. You are a minister on the team! We would like you to talk to him."

I went over to an elderly gentleman who was wearing a clerical collar. We began to talk, and he told me that he was Edward C. Cooper, archdeacon from the Episcopal Church of Guatemala. He had been a missionary for many years, and he was leaving the next day to go back to Guatemala. More than ninety years old, his sight was almost gone, and a handsome young man, whom he had led to Christ, was with him as a guide. "I wanted to hear Billy Graham," the clergyman said. "And when he gave that invitation tonight, I wanted to go forward. I am going back to Guatemala, and I want to be and do the best I can for my Lord in the years that I have left."

I thought to myself——I'm supposed to counsel him? I didn't, but we prayed together: "Oh, God," I prayed, "don't ever let me get to the place where I don't need a second touch, a third, a fifth, or a hundredth, of your Spirit!"

Some of us are looking back to the days when we sat in seminary with hearts aflame; but somehow the flame has died. What would happen if to the maturity, the quickened social conscience, the experience with people, the breadth of knowledge and learning, was added a rekindled flame? God would breathe again.

I am most concerned that my message may sound like, "Let the evangelist preach; let the activist march; let the charismatic pray; and let the academician mix in a little bit of everything. If we can just up the treble and down the bass, we'll have the sound for the 70's." But we are not God's sound engineers, are we?

I don't think God is saying, "Each of you do your own thing." I think he is saying, "It's time to turn and start doing *my* thing." Take a gospel that is true. Take a love that has presence, and take the power that belongs to God alone. Turn the keys. Open the lock. Go through the door, and he will be with you.

CHAPTER 5

EVANGELISM AND THE CITY

by the Reverend Tom Skinner

The Reverend Tom Skinner was born in Harlem in 1942. For some time he was the undisputed leader of the Harlem Lords, a street gang. In the short period since his conversion, thousands of people have come to know Jesus Christ through his ministry. Mr. Skinner is chairman of the board of Urban Ministries, Inc., a publishing firm specializing in educational materials for the black church.

5

I want to speak with you from my heart to yours about what I believe to be some very crucial issues of our times. I regret that we won't be able to have dialogue; that's how you really get at things. Lecturing, preaching, and even writing must move to some sort of interaction. I hope the day will come when dialogue becomes a regular feature of our church services. In dialogue sermons, the congregations can get at you. It's important to be available in that way.

One of the things I am discovering as I travel around the country is that most church people today are theologically and spiritually illiterate. Part of this is the result of the lack of dialogue to clarify what we mean. Another thing I find is that communication is not so much what's being *said* as what's being *heard*. Everybody wears a different filter.

Let me give you an example. I want to make no bones about myself. I am a militant, I am radical, and I am committed to revolution——to the overthrow of the present system. Now all of you heard that differently. Some of you picture a guerilla running through the streets with a machine gun, mowing people down. When I made that statement, you thought of my black skin and my beard; you considered the militant way my words come across, and a picture flashed before you of a guy ready to lead people in burning buildings. That's the filter you wear. Since we all hear things differently, dialogue becomes necessary to clarify what we mean by what we say.

It is so difficult to put evangelism into perspective because people filter that word, too. Evangelism means different things to different people. Perhaps the only way we can properly understand what evangelism means is to put it in the context of how it lives in situations we face, especially in our urban centers. We must try to come to grips with God's purpose for the church, to see what evangelism does within that purpose, and to visualize the nature of the world in which evangelism must be carried out.

Of prime importance is the need to understand who the church is. The biggest problem we face within the church is trying to be the church without a clear definition of the nature of the church. Who are we? We try to *do* evangelism without a clear understanding of what evangelism is, and we try to do this in the world without understanding what the world is really like. We must understand the nature of the world in which God has called us to be his witnesses. To clarify this, I would like to try to put into focus what I consider to be the issues of our cities today. As we sing "Lord, walk the crowded streets again," do we really understand what this would mean? Since the Lord can walk only through us, I wonder if we would be willing, in the name of Jesus, to walk the crowded streets.

People were attracted to the city at one time because the vast metropolis offered hope. That is what the city was: a place of hope and economic opportunity. The city became "hope" especially in the early stages of this country's industrial revolution. As industry began to boom, the United States went through a renaissance when the cities attracted people for job opportunities. Many immigrants, seeking to find a better way of life, migrated to the cities of America. Thus, the city became a great melting pot. Here was the place where all kinds of ethnic groups, economic groups, and people with diverse cultural idiosyncrasies could mesh into the vast city where opportunity awaited.

It was no accident that the Statue of Liberty was placed in the harbor of New York signalling, "Give me your tired, your poor, your huddled masses yearning to breathe free, the wretched refuse of your teeming shore." But while Miss Liberty stood facing Europe, greeting the world coming toward New York——toward America and the large cities—— Harlem saw only her back. While the American city became the place for immigrants to find opportunity, it turned its back on the people who were already here——our Indian brothers and sisters, our black brothers and sisters. The comforting words "Give me your tired, your poor, your huddled masses yearning to breathe free" were——and are—— not for them. Our Indian brothers and sisters and our black brothers and sisters are not free in 1973.

Immigrants of the nineteenth century who came hearing these words were affluent within seventy years. Because of the industrial revolution, they became the middle class in America, and soon this group of people, the pawns of the industrial revolution, began to sap the city of its resources. They were educated there, found their job opportunities there, raised their families there, saved their money there, and made their investments there. But after they achieved af- fluence, they abandoned the city. Slowly they began to move out to the bedroom communities——to suburbia. So often today, the people who sit on the city councils live in the suburbs. Those who sit on the boards of education of our cities make their homes outside the city limits. Their children do not have to attend those schools or feel the impact of those decisions. The people who run the city businesses and make the ultimate political and economic decisions do not have to live with their decisions. They live in suburbia.

The greatest tragedy, however, is that as these people packed up and left the city, so did the church! It ran, too. When we sing "Lord, walk the crowded streets again," we don't really mean that. Those are just words; we have for- saken the crowded streets of the city.

Crisis of identity

I think the main issues that we face in urban life today boil down to three. One is the crisis of identity. Large numbers of people are trying to come to grips with who they are. If you listen very closely to the "pop" songs of today, you will see that they are all raising the questions: Who am I? Why am I here?

A kid goes to his old man and says, "Dad, straight from

the shoulder. I want the facts of life. What's it all about?"

"Well, Son," Dad says, "it's all about going to school and getting yourself an education."

"What for, Dad?"

"Because, Son, you can get a better job."

"Why, Dad?"

"Well, you can make more money."

"Yeah, but what for, Dad?"

"Well, so someday you'll live in a better house, a better neighborhood, with a swimming pool, at least three cars in the garage, a television set in every room, and all. Uh, you'll be able to take a trip to Europe at least once a year for vacation. You'll make the proper investments in the right stocks, securities, and bonds."

"Yeah, but what for, Dad?"

"So that when you retire, Son, you will be able to retire comfortably."

"But why, Dad?"

"So that when you die, Son, you will leave something."

That's what it's all about! As cynical as it sounds, that is the kind of identity we have in this generation. We go to school to get a better education, to get a better job, to make more money, so we can retire comfortably, die, and leave something.

The church has not escaped: It has become infested with the same identity crisis. It measures success by those same guidelines. The "successful" church is the church with the biggest plant, the most affluent people, the most "successful" people. The successful pastor leads successful people. Even a lot of our seminary training is only to prepare us to help maintain the institution, or to be institutionally successful. And it follows that a great part of our money goes into brick and mortar. A building program is about the only time you can get church people "hopped up." Nothing else excites them as much. We sit down in pastors' meetings and hear, "We just finished putting in the latest accomplishment, a brand new $100,000 pipe organ."

Big deal! Those are our accomplishments because by not knowing who we are, we have become ecclesiastical "niggers." Because we haven't solved our identity crisis, we don't know what we're about, who we are, or why we exist. And that is the issue of our time: People are trying to come to grips with who they are. Who am I? What am I about? If the church is going to be on target in its message, it must come to grips with helping people discover who they are.

This is what Jesus was trying to say when he gave his inaugural address (Luke 4). He told us what he was going to be about when he stood up and said, "The Spirit of the Lord is upon me because he has anointed me to preach good news to the 'niggers.' "

I realize you have filters on when you read that word, so I will clarify. Poor people of Jesus' time were not simply people without money. Poor people were those who were regarded as scum. And they soon accepted that social definition of themselves. When a Roman drove his chariot down the road, he didn't bother to swerve the chariot around a poor person in the road; he ran right over him. The Roman saw the man in the road as little more than the dirt covering that road. The real tragedy was that the poor people began to identify themselves as dirt. That's what a "nigger" is—a person who allows somebody else to define him and then accepts the other's definition.

A nigger is a pastor who refuses to conduct his office according to the scripture but allows the congregation to define for him what a pastor ought to be. That's a nigger. A nigger is a minister's wife who can't wear the kind of clothes she wants to wear because "it's not what they expect of the preacher's wife." She's a nigger. Niggers are people who live their whole lives according to the definitions established by other human beings. Some pastors tell me, "I know I ought to be preaching what you're talking about. I can't because my board would ask for my resignation." If you have said that phrase, that makes you a nigger—because you are allowing somebody else to define what you ought to be. Jesus said, "I've got good news for niggers. I've come to tell you who you are. I've got good news for you." That is what the church must say.

At last, we live in a society where some people will stand up and say, "We're tired of being niggers." Yes, we're producing a lot of uppity people today who are tired of being defined. People are standing up on the college campus and saying, "I'm sick and tired of you defining me by my age. My age has nothing to do with what I know, with my intelligence, or my experience." That's what Paul was telling Timothy: "Don't be a nigger; don't let anybody despise thy youth." These niggers are saying, "We're tired of being niggers. Stop dealing with us according to age groups; deal with each one of us as a person."

Women are tired of being niggers. Women in this country have finally recognized that they are niggers. Women are standing up and saying, "I'm sick and tired of being defined as a sex object. I've got brains. I've got personality. I've got personhood and I want to be dealt with as a person." A bunch of uppity niggers!

Black people are standing up and saying, "You will now define me as an individual. I'm sick and tired of living by your definition of me. So from now on I'm not a 'negra'; I'm not 'colored folk'; I'm black, because 'black' is *my* definition. If you are going to deal with me, you're going to deal with me according to my definition, not yours." My Chicano brother stands up and says, "I'm not 'Mex'; I ain't 'spic'; I ain't 'Mex-American'! I'm Chicano! If you want to deal with me, you deal with me on *my* definition." All of these people are facing an identity crisis.

Crisis of community

Another problem we face in the urban setting is that of *community*. How can we build community? We have neighborhoods, but we don't have communities. Community happens when people become committed to each other. The word "community" has at least three words in it. From "com" we get the word "commitment." From "commun" we fashion "communion." Then the word "unity" is there. In the teeming metropolises of the world we are fighting to produce people who are committed to each other, who are in communion with each other, who have unity.

How do we build community? How do you experience community? For the past two years it has been my privilege to minister to the Washington Redskins. My argument with them has been that we must produce more than a professional football team: We must produce a group of guys who are committed to each other unto death—who become each other's brothers. Not just a team! Anybody can get out and become a team. The question is, "How do you become a community?" This is the essential question the church must ask. Out of all the institutionalism, the bureaucracy that we have created, the politics that we have become part of ecclesiastically, how do we produce community? How do we come together?

We salute the flag and mouth the words "one nation." Farce! I travel a lot around our country, and I speak in a lot of high school assemblies. Many schools still have morning exercises, the salute to the flag, the pledge of allegiance. It is amazing to see the thousands upon thousands of kids in this country who are not saluting the flag. Of course, their dumb parents and teachers think that the kids are anarchists, that the communists have gotten to them. We have a slick way in America of seeing a communist under every rock. Whenever anything goes wrong, a communist did it. Powerful people, those communists.

The reason these kids are not saluting the flag is not because they are anarchists or communists, but because they cannot say with integrity: "I pledge allegiance to the flag of the United States of America, and to the republic for which it stands." What *does* it stand for? "One nation under God." Now, where are we one nation? Where? Half a million of my Indian brothers and sisters locked up on reservations once owned this country. They were raped, pillaged, shot, driven from their land, and forced to live in isolated pockets called reservations. When we say that this is the land of the free and the home of the brave, it isn't the Indian brave we are talking about. Twenty-five million black people in this country have no upward social mobility. Five million Chicano brothers and sisters are not allowed to determine their own future. How can we say this is the land of the free?

This is one nation? Where? One percent of the population of this country has 43 percent of all the dollars. One percent of the population of America has 39 percent of all the common stock. One percent of all the companies in America makes 70 percent of all the products. This is one nation? No, my brothers and sisters, that's the greatest lie perpetrated upon the American people. We are a divided people; set against each other; divided into upper class, middle class, and lower class; divided into denominations. In spite of all the talk about ecumenicity, many of us are still exclusively committed to our own private aquarium while the ocean is there to fish in.

My question is: We know that Humpty Dumpty has fallen off the wall, but how are we going to put him back together again? The most segregated institution in American society is still the church. The most segregated hour in American society is still eleven o'clock on Sunday morning. One nation?

I have difficulty singing that hymn which says, "Onward, Christian Soldiers. All one body we. We are not divided . . ." because we *are* divided. Who is going to bring us together? How are we going to get community?

Crisis of power

The third crisis in our urban society is the issue of power. When I find out who I am, who my neighbor is, and understand my responsibility to my neighbor, where do I get the power to effect a change? How do I do it? Knowing right from wrong has never been a question in American life. We have generally been able to sort out intellectually what's right from what's wrong. But once I find out what is right, how do I do it?

At the very inception of this country, our forefathers were prone to making noble speeches about liberty, justice, peace, and tranquility. I have no difficulty believing that some of them were sincere in their expressions, but they couldn't pull it off. When Tom Jefferson wrote, "We hold these truths to be self-evident, that all men are created equal, that they are endowed by their Creator with certain unalienable Rights, that among these are Life, Liberty, and the pursuit of Happiness. . . ." and all that, I believe he was sincere. He just couldn't implement the idea. When Patrick Henry stood in the meeting that day with the British breathing down the colonists' backs, he made that very exciting speech. He said, "I know not what course others may take; but as for me, give me liberty, or give me death!" I have no problem believing that Pat Henry meant that: "Give me liberty, or give me death!" But it would have blown his mind if two dozen of his slaves had said, "Me too?" Because, you see, while Pat Henry was committed to liberty and justice for himself, he was not committed for his slaves——because he didn't have the power.

In our metropolitan areas today, people are powerless. People who live in the cities do not determine the future of the cities. They don't have any control over their circumstances. Everything is decided for them. They live in a powerless time, unable to shape their own futures. They can't even dream. This lack of impetus afflicts our whole nation. Since people have abdicated the right to dictate their own futures, they no longer know how to make determinations in these matters. Yet, people who own the system have allowed middle-Americans to attain a certain amount of the world's goods, of the benefits of the system. Now they use middle-America to maintain the system to oppress the city folk until middle-Americans no longer want to determine their own futures; they are satisfied with what they have. The man stands up and says, "In America, a vast number of people are the silent majority." Uninvolved, uncaring, they have never asserted themselves. They don't picket or demonstrate or anything like that. They're just ordinary home folk, this silent majority.

The dumb middle-American who is part of the silent majority never realizes the implications of this phrase. It reminds me of the preacher who stood at the funeral service one morning and said, "We have come to mourn our departed brother who has gone on to join the great silent majority." *Silent* people are *dead* people! The man in the city is trapped because decisions are being made for him without his being consulted, without the slightest concern about what he thinks or feels. So, because he feels powerless, he stands up and cries out, "Power to the people!"——because he needs something. Or he stands up and says, "Green power!" or "Black power!" or anything else because he senses his powerlessness. He is powerless to make decisions for himself; it's all decided for him.

Young people are sensing their lack of power. When they

go to school, "the plan" is outlined for them. Many times they have to study subjects totally useless for them, but they have to waste a part of their lives for "accreditation purposes." They can't determine their futures. They're powerless.

Education as a solution

The system has offered some possible solutions to the crises of identity and community and power. One solution offered is education. Spokesmen for the system said if we could produce a more informed society, our problems would be solved. What we have to do, they said, is to produce more educated people. In 1957, when the Russians put the first satellite into outer space, we in America got disturbed. "The Russians are going to beat us to the moon. Then we won't be *'numero uno'* anymore; we gotta be number one, so we've got to beef up our education so we can get to the moon first." We have this crying need in America to be number one. We've got to be on top. So what happened? We beefed up our education system to compete with the Russians, to get to outer space faster. Now we have the most conformed society in the history of man.

The average student who graduates from high school knows more about the physical laws of the universe than the greatest scientist did twenty years ago. Information in our country doubles every six years. Ten years from now it will double every three years. Last semester's textbook is already obsolete. Ninety percent of all the scientists who ever lived are alive right now. We are an informed society. The question is, my brothers and sisters, has all that information brought us together? Has it built community? Has it destroyed racism, poverty, oppression, hunger, war, militarism? Has it? No. That's the answer. You see, much of what passes as education today is not really education; it's indoctrination. We are not really collecting information about how to live.

When I graduated from school, I knew algebraic equations. I knew chemical equations. I knew something about grammatical structure and something about history, but I had learned nothing in formal education about how to live. I learned how to make a living, but not how to make a life. Nothing in the educational system taught me how not to be a bigot or how to destroy racism in my life. There was nothing there to help me deal with my hatred, my jealousy, or my pride.

We are making a moral shambles out of the system when all you have to do in order to be system-certified educated is just pass the test. Examination time? Just cram for it, pass it, and the system will let you through. Our system today is being run by people who passed the tests; so we drop bombs on people. It doesn't bother us that we destroy children, hospitals, people who can't lift a gun. We sigh, "War is hell," and the church gives divine credence. The church even supplies chaplains to the military to bless the pilots taking off with their deadly cargo. All are "educated" people.

Affluence as a solution

We hatched another solution for the cities: economic affluence. All we had to do, the system decreed, was produce enough of the world's goods; that would get us together. We are now the most affluent society in the history of man, but it hasn't brought us together. I used to think that affluence was the answer. All you had to do, I thought, was to put some money in a guy's pocket and that would solve the problems. We watched the kid in the ghetto pick up a brick and throw it through the store window. We saw him start a riot and figured the problem with that kid was he didn't have enough of the world's goods. If we had just supplied him with more of the world's goods, our problems would be solved. But that solution was dispelled, too.

One day we were standing on the riot-burned streets of Harlem. (We had riots there first.) We were loafing on the corner with nothing to do when all of a sudden smoke billowed over the horizon. We said, "Hey, the brothers over there are burning the neighborhood down!"

None of us lived over there, but we went to see what was happening. When we reached a nearby university campus, it was going up in smoke. "Hey, boys," we said, "the brothers on the campus are burning the place up." Then we saw the instigator. It wasn't some poor kid from the city or a Chicano or Puerto Rican or some black. Here was this upper-middle-class white kid burning the campus down. Now what was his problem? When they arrested him he had Carte Blanche, American Express, and Diner's Club cards in his pocket as well as charge cards to the city's major department stores. He was driving his first T-bird when the average poor kid was just trying to get his first bicycle.

This upper-middle-class white kid, too, was saying, "Let's burn the system." He was saying, "Affluence is not where it's at. While my Mom and Dad were out fighting to get in the social register, climbing to get status, working hard to make money to build that nice big house out there in suburban-ville, they never gave me any attention. They never gave me what I needed most——themselves. I didn't need their house, I didn't need their car, and I didn't need their money. I just needed *them*."

Who are the kids tripping out on drugs today? Poor kids? No. You folks didn't want to produce any laws against drugs ten years ago because all the people on drugs ten years ago were poor people in the city. You didn't care about them. As long as it was those poor "niggers" down there taking drugs, you didn't really care. Now your sons and daughters, and the youngsters of congressmen and senators, are tripping out on the stuff. Now we've got to pass laws. We have special drug programs in the church, special documentary films for P.T.A. meetings, and special lectures on how to tell if your kids are on the stuff.

Religion as a solution

The third solution offered was religion. We said we could solve everything if we could just make kids religious. Give them a song to sing, we said, a flag to wave, a creed to believe, and that would solve our problems. So we came up with good old Americanized religion. It went something like this: "I'm for God, country, motherhood, the girl back home, and apple pie." We Americanized religion, wrapping the American flag around God and making him the titular head of our system. We saluted the flag with "One nation under God." We embossed our money with "In God we trust," and somehow we fooled ourselves into believing that this was God's country.

Return with me now to yesteryear, when out of the past

comes a haughty law and order. George Washington prayed at Valley Forge, and Ben Franklin opened the first Congress with prayer. This is a God-fearing nation, we proclaimed. When? Have you ever checked out the theology of George Washington and Ben Franklin? They were both deists. According to the records, neither one of them believed in personal salvation through Jesus Christ. Neither one of them believed that "God was in Christ reconciling the world to himself." In fact, it was Ben Franklin who coined the phrase "Variety is the spice of life," and historians tell us he left enough illegitimate children in Paris to prove it.

And so, we perpetuate this mythology in our young people. We tell them that this is God's country. God has got his throne in America. This is devastating, for we get the impression that we can do anything we wish because we are a "religious" society. God is on our side, we claim, and we put bumper stickers on our cars: "For God and Country," as if the two go together. I suggest that a bumper sticker on your car might better read, "God *or* Country." There is no way you can convince me that God has put his stamp on this nasty, unjust, oppressive, militaristic, racist society in which we live.

God wants this system! There is cleverness in this proclamation. The people who own the system knew that the only way they could maintain oppressive control was to get us in the church to give it theological credence. They succeeded. We in the church produced a theology to maintain the system. Anybody who opposes us must be opposing God. Any nation that is against us has to be against God. Therefore, we are justified in dropping bombs on people, killing people, wiping people out. After all, we're doing it for God. We've got to stop those dirty, stinking communists because they're godless.

Could I suggest to you that if the way to stop communism is to use bombs and guns and bullets, then the way for the Chicanos and Indians to get their freedom in this country would be the same way? What's good for the goose is good for the gander.

We have also shackled religion to success. Today when we want to prove that Jesus Christ has validity, we go out and get people who are successful. We recruit a businessman who has made a million dollars to testify how Jesus helped him make a million. We get Miss America to tell us how God made her beautiful. We persuade an all-American all-star to tell us how God helped him score four touchdowns. He stands up and tells us, "I love God and country, and I play football." The perpetuators of the system are clever. They know they need our sanction in order to maintain their system.

Let me tell you that if God runs this system, God is the enemy. Because that would mean that God is responsible for slavery; God is responsible for the massacre of all those Indians; God is responsible for polluting his own air and his own water; God is responsible for dropping bombs on his own creation. That would make God the enemy.

Such is the nature of the world into which God has called the church to witness. Now we must come to grips with who we are and what we've got to do.

"As it is in heaven"

Jesus said to his disciples, "When you pray, here's what I want you to lay on the Father: 'Your will be done on earth as it is in heaven.' " This tells us that there is something going on in heaven, defining heaven as the sphere of influence which Jesus Christ controls. There is something going on in that sphere that is not occurring here on earth, and Jesus wants it to happen on earth. The function of the church—the answer to what's happening in our cities and what's happening all over America—is to assist God in producing a community of people who are live models on earth of what is happening in heaven. Then any time folks want to know what is going on in heaven, all they would have to do is check with us.

That is what I believe God has in mind for the church. The church is supposed to be a live model on earth of what is going on in heaven. How does that happen? Here is where evangelism has to come into focus. The kingdom of God is all about what needs to occur in our society. Jesus Christ came and said, "Repent, the kingdom of heaven has arrived." If the kingdom of heaven has arrived, what does it look like? How do I know it has arrived? I hear the preacher pronounce from the pulpit, "The kingdom of heaven has arrived." With my skeptical mind I say, "Where? Where? Show me!" In the inner-city slums, folks living with rats and roaches, police brutality, and slum landlords say, "Where is the kingdom? Show it to me!" "Come to church on Sunday," you say, "and we'll show it to you."

So I walk into your palaces, into your multimillion-dollar church buildings, your educational wings, and your fellowship halls. You say, "This is the kingdom." I see the results of millions of dollars poured into your brick and mortar— your empires—and I know back on my block there are people worried about tomorrow morning's breakfast. You build these fantastic buildings when there are people who have nothing to eat, and you say, "The kingdom has arrived"?

You cannot have a new community without having new folks. It is at this point that a divisiveness begins within the church. That is the whole point Jesus was trying to make with Nicodemus. Nicodemus came to Jesus and said, "Rabbi, we know that you are a teacher come from God because no man could pull off the things that you're pulling off except that God be with him."

He said "we" meaning that "we've discussed you back in the Sanhedrin council. Your name has been put on the agenda of numbers of meetings, and we've discussed you. We've discussed this young, radical preacher in town, and we all agree that you've got a message and that God's got his hands on you: blind people seeing, dead people coming alive, lame people walking. We think it's out of sight. The only thing that we object to is that you're doing it outside the system. You're not a member of our council. We haven't ordained you. We didn't lay hands on you yet. All we're asking is that you recognize that we've got the power. All we're asking is that you join us, for we could give you a base from which to operate. After all, you're a descendant of Abraham and we're descendants of Abraham; you're a Jew and we're Jews. You believe in the God of Abraham and we believe in the God of Abraham. That's a lot of things in common! Now you talk about this thing called the kingdom, and we talk about social reformation. It's just a matter of semantics and we ought to get together."

But Jesus said, "Now, Nicodemus, I don't want you climbing the wall when I lay this on you, but except a man be reborn, he can't see the kingdom I'm talking about."

Nicodemus was one of these liberal cats trying to question him because he was not like all the other guys. You understand there is a big divisiveness in the church over liberalism and conservatism. We black people got hoodwinked over that. We have a problem with the conservatives. If a man was theologically conservative, he felt he had to be politically conservative. He used his theology to oppress us black people politically. So even though we believed in the God he believed in and we both believed in salvation through Jesus Christ, we couldn't associate with this fundamentalist-conservative because he oppressed us.

When we went over to our liberal friend, we found he didn't quite believe all that the conservatives believed about the Bible being the word of God, the virgin birth, and all that stuff. He was more socially aware. He was the kind of cat who was interested in social reform. He wanted to change things, to have people to his house for dinner, you know.

What I found out is that there is really no difference between the conservative and the liberal—except their theology. Both of them want to run the system. The liberal is committed to the system, and the conservative is committed to the system. The only difference between the conservative and the liberal, the only reason they are fighting, is because they are fighting over who will control it. Neither one of them plans to change it.

About nine years ago, the religion department of a university in Richmond, Virginia, invited me to visit. The guys who ran the department there were theologically liberal cats who got together and worked their way into power. They wanted to get all the "fundies" out. Now, anybody who has a theological attitude different from theirs can't get on the campus!

The conservatives do the same thing. What they say is, "We are in control." While they talk about freedom, liberty, and all that, what they mean is "the freedom to have *our* way." What we must learn is that a conservative is a system man, a liberal is a system man, and the kingdom of God is committed to building a community that is diametrically opposed to that system.

That's what Jesus was trying to get Nicodemus to understand. "I ain't on your side, and I ain't on the Romans' side. The only difference between you and the Romans is that you all just want to fight over who's going to be in control."

You have to be reborn. And what Jesus was saying to Nicodemus was, "You cats are out there trying to build a new society without recognizing that unless you build a new man, you can't have a new community. You have to remake man; the issue lies there. Man must become a new person with new values, and a new system has new priorities." That is what Jesus was saying when he said, "Repent, for the kingdom has arrived." He was saying, "Repent. There are new priorities and new values. A new system has arrived. And it's personified in me."

Except a man be reborn, except he adopt the life-style of Jesus, except he allow the common clay of his humanity to become saturated with the life of Jesus Christ, he cannot become a new person. You can reform him so that he stops doing one thing and starts doing another; you can educate him so he gets increased information; you can change his poverty to affluence; but you do not change the man.

Because we do not have a bunch of remade men, we have people running our society today who have no values, no morals, and no ethics. This whole system is committed to one big success, and it doesn't care how success is achieved. Because of this loss of values and because people are not reborn, we are not sensitized. We don't care anymore in America. Because we are not reborn, a Watergate can take place where White House aides break into the opposing party's office, forge letters, bug the phone, create lies— do all kinds of things, and the American people don't care. The people in the church don't care. It didn't change the way they voted because they accept those actions as something you've got to do. That's politics.

Some people accepted a $400,000 bribe. Did the people of the church get mad? Were there any prophets in the pulpits of America who stood up and spoke against Watergate, ITT, or Continental Steel? Has the church stood up and said that all these people are insane? The answer is no, because we do not yet understand that reborn people are sensitized. Reborn people are outraged when people act like pagans. And because many people in the church have not been reborn, they can't be outraged.

The church is the easiest institution in the world to join. The Masons will give you a harder time. Anybody can join the church. All this membership requires is that the guy is ready to obey the rules and regulations of the institution. He does not have to give any evidence that Christ has become Lord of his life. He does not have to give any evidence of being reborn. All he has to do is join.

There is a reason for that: We do not want to go through the process of insisting that to belong to the community of heaven, the kingdom called heaven, a man must be reborn—that would cut down on the empire we are trying to build as preachers. The "successful" church is the church with the most people. If you start insisting that people be reborn and give evidence of a reborn life before they become part of the church, we wouldn't have too many church members. And we can't do that; we've got the big building to pay for. The mortgage is heavy. We need all the money we can get.

It becomes very difficult for the church to go out in the world and insist that to belong to the community, to the kingdom, a man's life must be reborn. His spirit must be pervaded with the life of God as expressed in Jesus Christ, as demonstrated by his death on the cross, and as proven in his resurrection. We cannot preach that, because we have never sold it to the church. The church has never bought it. Or, it has bought only half of the package—that a man must be reborn to get a passport out of hell into heaven. We preach this thing that says, "Accept Jesus as *personal* Savior." This is a kind of prostitution gospel preached evangelistically, because to "accept Jesus Christ as my personal Savior" means simply that I have my sins forgiven and God gives me a passport out of hell to heaven. It does not hold me accountable for my life-style.

A man who accepts Christ as his personal Savior can cheat in his business and feel good about it because, after all, he is a Christian. We have never demanded a total change of life.

So when kids were marching to integrate schools, the people who blocked the doors had Bibles under one arm and waved flags with the other, while cursing at the kids. One newspaper reported that one of these men was nice enough to come down and pass out tracts to these little black kids, telling them they needed to be saved. It was those bigoted parents, standing in the way of those black kids, who needed to be saved.

We have not learned that there is no such thing as accepting Jesus Christ as *personal* Savior. The word is, "Confess with your mouth and believe in your heart the *Lord*, Jesus." (Romans 10:9) Because we do not preach the *Lordship* of Jesus Christ, we are not obligated to obey him. We preach him as Savior, but not as Lord. We receive people in the church who have accepted Jesus as personal Savior; then they have to spend twenty years making him Lord. There are special spiritual-life conferences for these folks so they can grow; whereas, the New Testament Christians preached Jesus as Lord in their evangelistic message. All they ever heard was, "You must respond to Jesus as Lord." Evangelism in this country has become, "Accept Jesus as your personal Savior so you won't die and go to hell." That is not the message of the scripture.

A man must be reborn if he is going to become a part of the new community. The churches ought to begin to insist on that. But with this desire to have such vast facilities, to have the semblances of what a church is supposed to have according to our cultural thinking, we need many people to join the church to pay for it. That is why such small percentages of the people in our churches really follow Jesus. We are committed to building empires and organizations, not the community that Jesus was talking about.

A fellowshiping community

This new community is a fellowshiping community. The word "fellowship" means exactly what it says—fellow ship, fellows in the same ship. Jesus said to his new community, "I've come to build a new set of rules I want you to live by. That is, that you love each other the way I love you." Then he told them how that love will behave: "There is no greater love than one man laying down his life for another one." So when we talk about fellowship, we talk about a group of people who are committed to each other unto death.

Now to show you how far off we are and how we have become so committed to the system, Jesus is talking about dying for each other and we are going around talking about, "to bus, or not to bus, that is the question." While Jesus is talking about dying, we are talking about busing! Don't you understand that when you and I are ready to die for each other, there will be no busing issue? We're not ready to die for each other. That's why we're not prepared to go to school with each other. Because we're not prepared to die for each other, we don't want to live next door to each other. Because we're not prepared to die for each other, you've got your daughter scared to death of me. He's talking of dying! Are the brothers in your church prepared to die for each other? In most churches I see, folks don't even *know* each other; how are they going to *die* for each other?

Going back to our edifice complex, we built these church buildings in the city, and we didn't want to give them up. But all the people in the church moved out to suburbia. So, every Sunday morning we drive in from suburbia, converge in our church building, and have a thing called worship, which lasts from 11:00 till 11:59, with one minute for chimes. Then we jump in our cars and we rush back out again. We never get to know each other.

We realize we are supposed to have something called fellowship, so adjacent to the sanctuary we have another building program, called Fellowship Hall. That is where we are going to have fellowship, supposedly. Generally this announcement comes at the end of the service: "Immediately after this evening's service we will retire to the Fellowship Hall for a time of fellowship." We have our fellowship, complete with Christian booze——punch and coffee. But we never understand that the crying need of our times is for a fellowship where people are committed to each other unto death, where people are prepared to lay down their lives for each other.

Acts 4:32 says, "The multitude of those who believed were of one heart and one soul. None of them said that that which he possessed was his own, but they had all things common." The community which Jesus is establishing says, "What's yours is mine, and what's mine is yours. We live in common." But you say, "That sounds like communism. What in the world does that have to do with the kingdom?" We don't have that kind of commitment to each other. We are bound by the American culture that says "Every man for himself"——rugged individualism. We hold ourselves up by our bootstraps. "What's yours is yours, and what's mine is mine. I've got mine; you get yours."

We have no sense of commitment to each other. We just don't care. And because we don't know what it means to have fellowship, we don't take down our walls. Fellowship means getting underneath each other's skins, hurting with each other, and bleeding with each other. If there is anything the church ought to be known as, it is the "fellowship of the hurt ones," a group of people who can hurt together, who can let their hair down together, who can bleed with each other. We cannot do that.

We are all committed to having big churches. We are not willing to go back to the New Testament where people grew up in smaller groups. People can't grow up in large fellowships; we grow up in small families. As long as we are in a big fellowship, I can snow you because you'll never get to know me. We like that——snowing each other. We don't ever have to be honest, and you'll never get to know what I'm really like.

If we start breaking down into smaller fellowships, I will be able to snow you for only so long. You'll have to start really knowing me. And I don't want you to know me, especially as a minister of the gospel, because we preachers, pastors, and evangelists have been hoodwinked into believing that we wear halos over our heads. That's why we adopt such pompous airs. We change the inflections of our voice, and we talk like preachers. We look like preachers. We like all that—priestly robes, clerical collars, and the crosses. We go for all the trappings because they set us apart. At the same time, they make us inhuman, because we are not expected to be human. We are not expected to make mistakes, and if we do we don't let anybody know. That's why some of us die from ulcers, because we have to keep everything in. We can't let anybody know how we really hurt. We can't let anybody see us the way we really are. We are expected, as preachers of the gospel, to be above the throng, above the average man—beyond reproach. I don't know about you, but I have clay feet right up to my navel!

And so we don't want anybody to get to know us. I look at a pastor, and I see a very pompous man who is above everything. He looks so perfect. That makes me feel sick, because I know I'm flawed, and I don't even think I can approach him. How would a perfect man understand something imperfect like me? How would a man who has never argued with his wife understand my problem? How many of you as pastors have never confessed to your people that you and your wife argue? No, you can't afford to do that.

Because we don't have fellowship and don't love each other unto death, we're divided. All we have is an empire called "church," an ecclesiastical gathering where we go through some motions.

A witnessing community

Out of that church is supposed to come a witnessing community. It says one thing loud and clear—over and over again. "Jesus is alive! Jesus is alive!" It speaks not just in its verbal witness; it witnesses by the demonstration of its life. Jesus is alive!

One of the things that turned me off to the evangelists of the church was I didn't believe them. The people who came to me and verbally expressed that Jesus saves—that Jesus is alive and that Jesus shed his blood on Calvary and rose again from the dead—were the same people who would deny me employment. These same people would not let me buy a home in any neighborhood where I could afford to live. They were the same people who kept their kids away from me. Their words had no witness because their life-style was diametrically opposed to what they verbalized.

The leaders of the church today have killed its witness. Instead of being the leaders, going out into the community, being salt and light, and representing the demonstration of God's life-style from heaven, we have ended up acting and living the same way as the world system. Since we are no different, our witness has no validity. If the church's witness for Jesus is to have validity, its life-style must say, "Jesus is alive!"

That brings us to the problem of how this witness can be accomplished. When Walter Rauschenbusch wrote his paper entitled "Christianity and the Social Gospel" in 1906, it produced a dichotomy in the church. One group said, "Our witness is to go out and save souls—to tell men to repent and turn to God, to tell them to turn from hell to heaven." Another group says, "No, we've got to feed some hungry people. Folks' bellies are empty out there. Naked people need clothes. People don't have shelter. We've got to go out and do that thing." So they argue. And they both end up being wrong.

One group only wanted to save something called "my soul," as if it were some special compartment in me that needed to be saved. But that group didn't care about my body or mind. The other group just wanted to feed my belly. It had no concern about my spiritual needs—the rest of me. When Jesus said, "What does it benefit a man if he gain the whole world and lose his soul?" the word "soul" meant "being." Jesus wants to save all of me, not some part of me. What must be produced is a new witness, a witness which comes in the name of Jesus and says that the healing of Jesus is for the totality of man—to heal mind, body, and spirit. He has come to take all of you and put you together.

That is fundamentally what Paul was trying to say when he said to the church at Ephesus, "Put on the whole armor of God." The Roman soldiers had all kinds of protection for various parts of their body, but when they ran into battle, the separate pieces of armor were very loose and kept them from being agile. They invented the "girdle" to be worn around the center of the man's body. The straps on it were connected to all his equipment, holding it together so he could run with agility. Paul understood what psychiatrists are beginning to understand today: Man is mind, body, and spirit. But these elements shoot off in different directions, and we need something at the center of our lives to get it all together. Paul says, "Have your loins, the center of your being, girded with truth." The question is: Who is the truth?

Jesus said, "I am the truth." The witness of the church should be: We have a girdle that can put man together. The witness of the church is to go out and demonstrate that it is together——that God has made us whole men and whole women. That witness will be done through preaching, through television, radio, passing out tracts, and so forth. I think that's great, but the real witness of the church has to be *demonstrated*.

In the black community, Chicano community, and Puerto Rican community of each teeming city, your tracts and literature distribution just wouldn't do it. You are going to have to go down there, be real, hurt, and bleed with us. In other words, you must pay your dues. Does the church want to pay its dues, or are we still committed to the clean-cut, nice things?

We like to witness to nice people: none of those long-haired hippies, none of those flower people, none of those drug addicts, alcoholics, and prostitutes. We don't need them. Let's get the word out to these good, clean-cut, American kids. Let's get the word out there to nice, clean-cut suburbia where people are *nice*. After all, there's prestige out there. You might be fortunate enough to witness to a successful businessman, and how *nice* it would be to have him in the church.

Isn't there a word for our prostitute sisters down in the red-light district? Don't you want to go live with them? "Why, we can't go down there, we might lose our testimony." That's the problem——we're so busy trying to save our testimony that we never give it. When we talk about witnessing and about going into the world, we are talking about the church being held on the football field. We are talking about the church being on the golf course, in houses of prostitution, in bars, discotheques, and homes, and on the street. We are talking about the church being in Congress, and God knows we need it in the White House. We don't understand that as witnesses we are supposed to infiltrate the world. That is what God has called us to be: fifth columnists, saboteurs.

We are saboteurs, fifth columnists bent on infiltrating the world's system, because this whole system is evil. It lies in the hand of the Evil One——controlled by Satan. But God has called us to overthrow the world by our witness and by our life-style, and that includes the American system. We will not accept that the American system also lies in satanic hands. We believe it lies in God's hands. That is why we refuse to prophesy to it. God wants us to prepare to go into every area of the world to represent the kingdom of God in the world system. But, instead of the church producing representatives from heaven to the system, it has ended up receiving representatives from the world to the church.

When we choose our board of elders, board of deacons, stewards, people for the powerful positions in our church, what kind of laymen do we pick? We pick successful laymen, successful businessmen, successful executives—men with money. It never occurs to us that such a man just may represent the system. Maybe he is more interested in perpetuating the business of which he is an executive than perpetuating the kingdom of God. If there ever came a choice of whether the church would survive or his business would survive, he would choose his business, because he's committed to the system.

Since we have the system represented in the church, the church has never taken a stand on the right issues. The church has never taken a stand on racism because the businessmen of the church would have to knuckle under, and the real estate people at the church would have to yield. Since they control the church, write the preacher's checks, control his salary, he can't afford to buck the system. Many of us as pastors are employed in the church as people who are literally committed to the system and not to the kingdom. The people from whom we collect our paychecks control what we preach, what we say, and even what we will stand for.

The church is a kingdom separated from the world. Its life-style and philosophy are diametrically opposed to the world system. This separated group of people produces mature soldiers of the cross to go into the world system and represent the kingdom—to commit spiritual sabotage on it for Jesus. That is our witness. Yet, when people in the church begin to stand up and speak out against the system and launch attacks against it, we criticize them in the church.

When Martin Luther King, Jr., started marching against the racism of the land, the church stood up and cried, "Why doesn't he just go preach the gospel? Why does he get involved in all that?"

Why? Because that's where the church is *supposed* to be. The gospel you were preaching or hearing was not addressing itself to the hot issues. That's why he had to go out there. Your gospel wasn't *the* gospel. "Why didn't those people stop preaching about Vietnam, Cambodia, or Laos, and preach the gospel?" Because the gospel you were preaching wasn't stopping the bombing, that's why. That's where the church is supposed to be.

It was the function of a prophet to sit at the king's gate. When the king made a decision that was not of God, the prophet went out and stood up against him and told the people to withdraw their support. When the king made a decision that was of God, the prophet went out and urged the people to support it. There are no prophets sitting at the king's gate today. There are no prophets in the country standing up and saying to our leaders, "Thus saith the Lord." John the Baptist has now become "chaplain" in Herod's palace instead of "prophet."

Now that the system realizes we have a theology that can help the system, we are given some prestige. When a senator or somebody invites us to his house, we talk about that for days——"The preacher was invited to the senator's house." You stand in such awe of the senator it never occurs to you that he is supposed to stand in awe of you as a minister of the gospel! We're such niggers, so happy to be accepted by these folk, so awed that they've given us an opportunity to get next to them, that we have no prophetic word for them. I am a minister of the gospel of Jesus Christ——the highest calling in all the world——and a senator of the United States has to stand in awe of my calling. My calling supersedes his. That is the witness.

Niggers are prestige-conscious because we have always been denied prestige. So when we get it, we don't want to say anything that will lose it. It's the same thing that we black people went through for years. We were so happy to be around white folks that we just "yes, sir'd" and "no, sir'd" you to death. On a beautiful day with not a cloud in the sky, you'd come up to us and say, "Boy, it's snowing today." "Yes, sir, Boss, it is." We weren't a witnessing community.

A discipling community

Finally, this new community has to be a discipling community. It must take the people who respond to its witness and are reborn into the kingdom, and it must disciple them ——raise them in the faith. It is one thing to produce in a maternity ward; it is quite another to raise the kid after he's born. Much of evangelism recently has been a vast maternity ward, nothing more. We end up with all these babies who never grow up.

I went to a thing in Dallas, Texas, called "Explo 72." It was the most exciting, and depressing, meeting I ever attended——exciting because more than a hundred thousand people from all over the country gave witness to Jesus Christ. About a hundred thousand people were trained to share their faith with other people. That was exciting.

It was depressing because we turned loose in this country a hundred thousand evangelists without any plan for follow-up. God's word will not be wasted, for many of these people will go back to their homes in the cities and their jobs and, through their literature and verbal witness, other people will come to accept Jesus and the new birth. But we did not produce an army of teachers to follow that army of evangelists! Within the next decade we will produce the most retarded generation of Christians in the history of the church. We will have all these spiritual babies running around starving spiritually, never growing up into what Paul calls the "full manhood and stature of Christ Jesus."

God's purpose is to produce a full-grown, spiritual being. The new birth is only one process on the way to that. We want to fill the church up with all these babies, but we don't want to take the pains of helping them grow up. You can not build vast empires for people to grow up in; people can only grow up in families. So, if we want to raise people, we will have to dismantle the structure of the church.

Our churches will have to start breaking up into smaller

groups. The pastor, who is supposed to equip the saints for the work of the ministry, will have to start enabling small group pastors to lead small groups. We pastors like to say, "God has placed on me the burden of ministering to 2,000 people. What a great burden! Sometimes I fall beneath the weight, and I get down on my knees and ask God. . . ." You know, we like that. It's a dumb, stupid prayer, because God never intended you to have 2,000 people in your ministry. God intended you to minister to a small group, and those members would minister to yet another group. Then those 2,000 people would be reached.

Meanwhile, you're probably not reaching anybody. No pastor can minister to 2,000 people; you're just kidding yourself. The best you can do is to deliver a good homiletical message to those people on Sunday morning. You can't raise 2,000 people in the twenty minutes, or forty-five minutes, you preach. We've got to stop kidding ourselves. Until a church has a strategy and everybody in that church is involved in breaking down into smaller families, the church will never raise discipled people. And that's where it's at!

We are hung up with this thing called "clergy" and "laity." God never created such a thing. God's function is to see that the people do the work; not to watch a performance on the platform. "But God says that I'm the shepherd of the sheep." Yes, but shepherds don't reproduce sheep——sheep reproduce sheep. God has not called you to do the reproduction. He has called you to equip people to reproduce other people to be witnesses. He has called you to send evangelists into the business world, into the entertainment world, into the sports world, into every walk of life.

Your job is to equip people to go out. You are to be the coach. Coaches don't *play* quarterback; they *coach* quarterbacks. That is why God has called you to the church. You have got to spend time pouring yourself into people. When we become pastors, we go out visiting the sick, we become janitors, money grubbers, and bookkeepers. We take communion to the shut-ins. Members of the congregation should be trained to do that. You should see that it happens. The president of General Motors does not make cars; he sees that they are made. The function of a pastor is to see that it happens, not to do it. That is what God has called us to.

We must become a new community, a reborn people, a fellowship of folk committed to each other unto death, and a community witnessing by its life-style. These are the issues in the world.

Jesus is alive. Let's make it plain, so there is no misunderstanding. When I say Jesus is alive, I do not mean the concept of Jesus is alive or the philosophy of Jesus is alive. *Jesus* is alive! The church must demonstrate by its life-style and as a discipling community that raises people in the faith.

You've got one obligation. You can totally reject what you've heard——make excuses——"That might work in an ideal situation, but in my church I can't do that." And that's a cop-out. If you believe that "to whom much is given much is required," you're obligated to go back to the vineyards that you labor in and *start making it happen*. God help you.

CHAPTER 6

EVANGELISM AND THE WHOLE PERSON

by the Reverend James B. Buskirk

*The Reverend James B. Buskirk is director of a new ministry
in creative evangelism, Motivation for Ministry. A veteran of
seventeen years in the United Methodist ministry, he holds
the B.A. degree from Millsaps College, and the B.D. degree
from Candler School of Theology. Mr. Buskirk is the first
incumbent of the Chair of Evangelism recently established at
Candler School of Theology.*

What a rich diversity we have been given under the theme, "Evangelism in the Life of the Church." Every contributor has implied that evangelism relates to more than initial commitment. It extends beyond the first phase of a consciously redemptive relationship. The work of evangelism is more than a spiritual nursery. Christian evangelism relates to the whole person and to his whole environment.

William Sloane Coffin reminded us that evangelism is social prophecy, that it relates to war, race, poverty, pollution—and the list could continue. With Leander Keck we learned that primary in evangelism is the act or the action of God. We looked at the contours of salvation with the rubric of apocalyptic freedom and, moreover, were encouraged in that the "Flesh," or historical Jesus, can become our "word," or message. James May showed that some of history's potent parallels to our present options in evangelism provide caution and compass. An evangelism adequate for today, Leighton Ford told us, will find expression in proclamation, presence, and power. The urban unrest and that of the world were reviewed by Tom Skinner through the crises of identity, community, and power. He brought the good news that community is possible where Jesus is alive, not the concept of Jesus, but where "Jesus is alive!" In that community we love one another enough to die for one another.

We ask now, as we focus on our local points of ministry, "How do we get it all together?" We have been ministered to at the cutting edge of concepts, and these have offered correction and direction. Now, how do we appropriate it all? How do we embrace the ideals and pull the actualities of our local church closer to them? What does this mean for "Evangelism in the Life of *Our* Church"?

Let us begin to outline the life-style of a church whose evangelism is not only aware of whole personhood but also actualizing whole persons. A model with some real clues is afforded us in the letter to Ephesus.

> Naturally there are different gifts and functions; individually grace is given to us in different ways out of the rich diversity of Christ's giving. . . . His "gifts unto men" were varied. Some he made his messengers, some prophets, some preachers of the gospel; to some he gave the power to guide and teach his people. His gifts were made that Christians might be properly equipped for their service, that the whole body might be built up until the time comes when, in the unity of common faith and common knowledge of the Son of God, we arrive at real maturity —that measure of development which is meant by "the fullness of Christ." (Ephesians 4:7, 11-13 Phillips)

Ministry to the inward person

First, let us claim the ministry of the grace of God to the inward person: "Grace is given to us in different ways out of the rich diversity of Christ's giving. . . . Some he made. . . preachers of the gospel [etc.]." What is this "grace"—this "gospel" or good news? It is the good news of God's affirmation, his acceptance of us. Now this is no bland approval that leaves us as we are. Acceptance does not mean that we are acceptable.

Who of us cannot really claim our guilt, our need, our sin? Who of us does not need real grace? Would any of us insist that we have done well as a parent? When I think that my children might best be enabled to understand relationship with their heavenly Father through the language of relationship in our family, I am quick to confess that my efforts have not matched my affection. We wonder if anyone in the poverty pockets of our cities could claim relationship with the Father because they have had contact with us. Would any nation in the world be more inclined toward Christianity because they have had dealings with the United States? I don't think any of us would say that we are not candidates for God's acceptance, his affirmation, his ministry of grace to the inward person.

How great is our need for God's forgiving acceptance— and if we cannot acknowledge that need, is not the need even greater? This is not to imply that his acceptance completely releases us from guilt, but such affirmation does keep guilt from immobilizing, paralyzing us. We can begin again and continue where we have relationships.

Let me relate this idea another way. I am usually very "Christian" when I watch television with my family. That is, they can watch just about whatever they like, so long as it's not "Lucy" or "Carol Burnett." Those are just not my programs. Women may be their target audience, so I asked my wife, Nancy, how one would relate to those programs. "Oh, that's easy," she said. "They're always coming off 'all thumbs' and 'left arms,' and it's therapeutic to see them in such dilemmas rather than being there yourself." Now I can identify with the all-thumbs, left-arms feelings, can't you?

At this point Bruce Larson in *No Longer Strangers* helps us to see grace. His attention was claimed by the graffiti on a subway wall in New York. Some of it was obscene, some sad, and some funny. From the mouth of an austere, proper, older gentleman on an advertising poster, someone, a small boy perhaps, had sketched the phrase, "I like grils." Underneath, someone else had written, "It's girls, stupid, not grils." Below that still another person had added, "But, what about us grils?" The good news is that "grils"—all thumbs and left arms included—are accepted by the grace of God.

To receive this, to affirm our affirmation, is a primary step toward becoming whole persons. No doubt such a ministry of affirmation comes through best in relationship, in the collective. What an opportunity for the church, although it is not always there that we see it. Such grace is in a college fraternity, Roy Burkhart related when I heard him preach during my seminary days. This is the account as I still recall it.

When preaching on a campus, Roy was invited to come to a fraternity house to rap with the fellows. They sat in a circle in the big den, risking some honesty, and then there was silence. For thirty seconds, which constitutes a long time, there was silence. "I almost broke the silence," Burkhart said, "but fortunately did not."

A young man spoke up and said, "I ought to say something, but I'm afraid."

"Afraid?" said Burkhart. "Why?"

"I'm afraid you'll laugh at me," the man replied.

"Can you afford to be laughed at?" continued Burkhart.

"I don't know," said the college man. "I've been laughed at before and it isn't fun."

Another silence followed and someone suggested maybe Bill would rather not share.

"Yes," Bill said, "I want to say this. You guys talk about the fraternity being a home away from home. Well, it's my first home like this. You see, all my life—well, I've just been a 'nobody.' I was reared in a small community some distance from here. I was born out of wedlock. My father left my mother when he learned that she was expecting. A few hours after my birth, my mother took her own life. I was reared in that small community by my grandparents. Everybody knew who I was. I was 'that boy'—a 'nobody.' But here I belong; on the campus I'm a 'frat man.' My studies—well, it all makes a lot more sense now. Because of what you guys mean to me—well, I wanted you to know. Now that you know it all—maybe I'll be a 'nobody' here. It's O.K. I still wanted you to know."

"Then," said Burkhart, "I saw one of the greatest things I've ever seen." The president of the fraternity jumped up, crossed the room, clasped Bill's hand, pulled him up from the couch. He embraced him as he said, "Man, it doesn't matter to us where you've been; the thing that counts with us is you, man. We know you and we like you!" All the fraternity brothers tried to get to Bill. They tousled his hair and slapped him on the shoulder.

"I saw," said Burkhart, "broad-shouldered, bearded young men embrace each other. I saw acceptance and affirmation!"

Now that is what the church ought to be, as her best has been, and is called to be. Thus she claims the ministry of the grace of God to the inward person. This is an initial step toward producing whole persons.

Outward thrust of mission

With the inward ministry alone we can become harmfully introspective. A church whose evangelism is contributing toward whole persons will include in its life-style the outward thrust of mission.

"Messengers," "prophets," "preachers of the gospel," and "those who guide and teach" are listed by the writer of Ephesians. If we agree that evangelism does not simply run a spiritual nursery, then one of these persons is not necessarily any more the evangel than the other.

Why are these functions given? "His gifts are made that Christians might be properly equipped for their service. . . ." The Revised Standard Version translation for "service" has "ministry." I like the fact that we are accepting the idea that laymen are ministers, that ministers are enablers and equippers. As all Christians are called to be evangels, so are all Christians called to "ministry," and that has an outward thrust. Some might argue that the writer of Ephesians by "service" refers to ministry within the fellowship. In either case, the comprehensive Pauline concept is that of world mission.

What does "ministry" include for your church? Can you name six specific, concrete, good things that are happening in your community beyond the walls of your church that would probably not be happening if your church were not there? Can you name twenty, twelve, or two such things that any pagan could recognize? If your church had to receive its funds by government appropriation and only such community ministries could justify your request for funds, what would you list? If asked to list the things within the walls of our churches, the list would be much longer. I don't mean to discredit those activities, but the best advertisement your church has is what it is doing in the community beyond the walls.

A small boy wrote on his school chalkboard, "Sammy Jones is the best kisser in school!" He was promptly punished. On the way to school the next morning his girl friend said, "Sammy, I guess you learned it doesn't pay to misbehave."

"Yes," he answered, smiling, "but I learned something else too—it sure doesn't hurt to advertise!" Your church's ministries may be her best advertisement.

Elton Trueblood enables us to grasp a balanced perspective when in *The New Man for Our Time* he demonstrates that Christian devotion without ministries offers roots without fruits, and ministries without devotion propose fruits without roots.

We include the outward thrust of ministry, then, for the sake of wholeness. Is there any better motivation for ministries than gratitude for grace? This is a healthy sequence, but let us not imply that it is the only sequence.

For others, ministries may precede grace. There are many in our culture who are disciplined, attractive, dependable, successful persons more aware of their strengths than their weaknesses. Their image of themselves resembles Dietrich Bonhoeffer's "strong man" more than it does the man of crises who could hear the invitation to surrender. These persons, although they would not readily express their own needs, can recognize needs in the community or a neighbor's need. I contend that it is a viable approach to invite them to join others in ministering to such recognized needs. After exposure to others who have joined God in ministry and to such ministry, it may be a clear option for such persons to commit more of themselves to the God they have experienced in mission.

The traditional sequence is a general theological understanding of God and ourselves. We commit ourselves and then try to particularize in our own lives. This approach to persons of strength is the opposite sequence. First, the particular is experienced; then a more total commitment may be made. I believe it is good news for the "strong person" that God wants to employ our strengths as well as forgive our weaknesses.

Maybe we ought to look at new forms in the church. Some worshipers want to celebrate redemptive change, and some want to celebrate law and order and things as they are. This idea may not be new in concept, but it is new in actuality in our churches.

The church that extends its ministry of grace to the outward thrust of community mission has, in this authentic life-style, a more comprehensive evangelistic appeal. Such is evidenced at Trinity United Methodist Church in Atlanta. Students in the Doctor of Sacred Theology program and I toured Trinity with its pastor, the Reverend Ken Jones, and this church in mission almost overwhelmed us.

How does one describe such a church? Do you begin with the sanctuary of this historical site of Methodism in Atlanta? It is in ill repair. Who could forget the big fissure in the center of the roof from which debris has fallen during worship?

Is Trinity, on the other hand, seen more authentically when you look at her ministries? Ken Jones could tell us of the meager beginning with almost no resources available— the lawn care ministry with push lawn mowers and boys from the street who needed work. Would we be more interested in Trinity's ministry to Grady Hospital's overflow, or the drama group at Trinity? Perhaps we would be more interested in the Parish House with surplus food, medical assistance, counseling for those who could not otherwise afford it, and legal aid. In other words, we could see the focal points of that particular community of need in urban Atlanta. These ministries are no less exciting than those through Trinity for senior citizens, "the left-overs and the left-outs." Their children's programs are ambitious and include a children's camp, leased from the government.

Trinity is in the business of making people whole, by beginning where they are. This focus on persons' needs has many products, one of which is a serendipity in evangelism.

Who could miss this serendipity watching a group of older youth, some of whom have been redeemed from drugs by Trinity's superb ministry to that culture? Their choice of ministry was to instruct, to work with, a class of retarded children. Those whose minds might have been scrambled by drugs have a patience, a love, a skill with the retarded that overcomes you.

In fact, at Trinity it is difficult to tell who are those who minister and who are those who are ministered unto. That is perhaps ministry at its reciprocal best. And perhaps that is why Trinity's evangelistic appeal is greatest at the point of attracting persons who are looking for that life-style, a place to minister—a handle.

Trinity is not "bugged" by that fissure in the roof. She has something to celebrate, and the place of that celebration does not have to be perfect. At Trinity, men are more important than mortar, and new bridges to the community more crucial than new brick. God may inspire some of the rest of us to provide the new materials needed while Trinity ministers.

Trinity's choice is also ours. She could have looked at her fissure and her superb history and continued to become a monument. Instead she chose ministries. Your church and mine are on their way to one life-style or the other: monuments or ministries! The outward thrust can make the difference. I do not believe that there are any other directions right now.

Unity without uniformity

How do we achieve, in our church's life-style, the ministry of grace to the inward person and the outward thrust of ministries? How do we avoid polarization on the one hand or conformity to one pattern on the other? There is a further word for us in Ephesians. ". . .There are different gifts and functions; individually grace is given to us in different ways out of the rich diversity of Christ's giving. . . . His gifts unto men were varied." This offers unity without uniformity.

I like the change in the United Methodist local church from the Official Board to the Administrative Board. The Official Board suggests to me those who say yes and no. The new name implies those involved in administration, a form of ministry.

At one church where I served as student pastor we had an Official Board. We had not really claimed unity without uniformity. After several years of transporting people to church in several private cars, a wonderful thing happened. Mr. Claude Hinton suggested that we needed a church bus.

"I want to be sure," he said, "that children whose parents do not bring them to church will have a way to attend." He suggested that although he usually traded cars every two years, he would continue to drive his present one. In this way he could buy a small bus for his church.

"What do you think, pastor?" Mr. Hinton asked.

"Great," I said, "but you'll have to put your name on a list. It takes five weeks to get that kind of bus."

"Oh," he said, "I've had my name on the list a month already, and it's supposed to be here next Sunday."

Sunday the bus was there. Mr. Hinton was to give me the keys after morning worship. I preached a very brief sermon and invited the people to meet me outside the sanctuary.

Can you imagine the joy Mr. Hinton experienced in giving those keys? By the time he put them in my hand, the children had read the sign on the bus, "Hinton Memorial Methodists Welcome You," and realized Mr. Hinton was giving the bus. They ran to him, pulled him over, and began hugging his neck. Then others got in on it. There were red lipstick smears on Mr. Hinton's cheek and forehead that I don't think just his nieces put there. He turned a becoming pink and said, "Ladies, I'll have another one here next Sunday!"

Two men on the Official Board, however, got out a little late. Upon seeing the bus one elbowed the other and said, "Would you look——they've done something else without bringing it before the Official Board!" And the bus was a complete gift! Mr. Hinton's unique and generous response to a need that he saw is a real clue to unity without uniformity.

In Motivation for Ministry missions we take a survey during worship. The congregation completes anonymously this sentence: "The specific need I see in my community to which I wish lay persons were ministering is. . . ." Their replies are sorted by topics, and the different subjects are posted on meeting room doors. After the hour of worship, members of the congregation select the ministry that appeals to them. In this way, ministry groups are born, and existing ministries find additional personnel. The collective or group strength is maintained in the church scattered, the church in ministries.

Evangelism leads to mission, and mission may well become evangelism. It did in Malesus, Tennessee. Recognizing needs in the community, one group focused on the nearby Tennessee Sheriffs' Boys' Farm. They found a most urgent need for remedial reading. Men from the church met boys at the farm in the evenings and "one on one" assisted them in reading skills.

One of the boys asked an adult, "Why do you do this?"

"Because I love you," the adult answered.

"And why do you love me?" the youth continued.

"I'm a Christian," said the adult, "and love is what it's all about."

The next question from the boy was "What does it mean to be a Christian?" The adult was sincere and honest enough to tell the lad what he could then, and he sought help before he met the boy again. The point is, that adult had earned the right to tell that boy what it meant to be a Christian.

This all happened because a church discovered unique needs in the community and created ministries to relate to those needs. Because the gifts of persons are varied, different groups focus on different needs. There can be unity without uniformity.

A "people" thing

If our church takes on this life-style of evangelism for the whole person, one undergirding awareness keeps the total process valid and truly redemptive. Ministry (or evangelism) is a "people" thing! *Individually grace is given....* His gifts unto *men. . . .* His gifts were made that *Christians. . . ."* These words underscore that this is a "people" matter, and this fact suggests two things to me. People are too precious to be manipulated. Persons can change if they wish when given redemptive support.

With regard to the first, I confess that once I thought evangelism was something you "do." I was skilled at convincing the legitimizers in a parish and through them getting things "done." This is not to suggest that one should be oblivious to power structures. On the contrary, most of us need to see that redemptive change can come not only through altars but also through city halls. Yet, ministry is not just something you do or get done. Ministry's core is "becoming." Structures often need to be changed to free people to "become." This process is indeed evangelism. Evangelism, rather than manipulation, supports and enables persons who wish to change redemptively.

We are not frozen even in our uniqueness. Unity without uniformity can be expanded. Enlargement is not without threat, as I learned at Atlanta's East Lake United Methodist

Church. I chose to work there one quarter in my doctoral program as a parallel effort to a course in urban training. When I chose it, someone suggested it was a good assignment since I was originally from Mississippi. I didn't think I liked that remark, but I understood it better when I got to East Lake. The church consisted of about fifty whites and three hundred blacks.

And what a church! On Monday evening they had study halls in the facilities. On Tuesday evening I helped in the remedial reading clinic. On Wednesday nights I coached basketball. This was only a part of their recreation program. On Thursday evening the youth had the "Circle of Love," a recreation and Bible study time of about two hours. On specific evenings at the church, with the aid of an Atlanta college, shorthand and typing classes trained women for better jobs. Previously equipped for little more than the work of maids, these women usually doubled their incomes, and their entire families felt the benefits.

Can you imagine worship at East Lake? It's celebration! That church had radically improved the life-style of its people.

Although I appreciated the ministries there, I was not without threat in my participation. I tried to play it adequate and secure, but they read me loud and clear. Yet, they were supportive in my struggle with change, and this is how they let me in on their awareness. I got out of my car one night, started for the church building, and from a crowd of boys I heard, "There he is, get him!" I was aware that I could not outrun them. I walked on hoping they were not talking about me. They charged up. Three grabbed my right arm and three grabbed my left. Then the largest put his big fist near my face and just as I was about to collapse, two fingers popped out of the fist making the peace sign as he said, "Peace, baby!"

The boys laughed and ran on toward the church. This was their way of letting me know they were in on my struggle. The joking and laughing was their way of joining me in a supportive way. Who of us does not need to risk growth? How redemptive is support in the process!

Note the limits, or are there any? The writer of Ephesians

refers to "real maturity—that measure of development which is meant by *'the fullness of Christ.'* " Even the sky is not the limit here. What good news addresses us when we are associated with someone clearly in that process of becoming!

At a laymen's conference at Lake Junaluska, I met a man who started discovering his whole person. "I have failed at everything," Pete said, "except maybe my profession." He is a skilled doctor. His father, however, had left his mother when Pete was just an infant, and Pete had failed at more than one marriage.

"I'm totally unworthy. How could anyone love me? I have only hurt everyone who tried," he continued. "I've gone through life just distributing garbage. I don't want it so, but I could never change all that and truly become a Christian."

It was a joy to share with him the good news that there is One who would share his life. In the strength of this relationship, those things inconsistent with wholeness could be phased out and those things added that were consistent and whole.

Certain persons at the conference provided the kind of support Pete needed to affirm this. He was there because a doctor friend whom he admired professionally and personally had shown him a life-style redemptively changing, discovering wholeness. This friend had invited and urged him to come to the conference as a personal favor.

In a small-group experience, Pete looked into the face of a lovely Christian woman with whom he prayed in silent, open-eyed prayer. As others were praying, this pure, beautiful woman affirmed him as a person worthy of her prayers and respect. A great layman at the crossroads in his own unique ministry shared his struggle with Pete and affirmed him by requesting prayers.

Before leaving, Pete claimed grace and began a remarkable process. He gave me a book and the inscription clearly portrays an image of himself. It was, "God loves you and I love you for helping to show me his way!" It was signed, "The Garbage Man."

I kept in touch with Pete. Once home he started correcting those relationships that suggested his crucial lack of wholeness. He took to lunch a colleague with whom he had competed unfairly in a professional way. Pete almost "blew the man's mind" as he asked forgiveness and pledged friendship.

Because Pete knew he would become what he gave himself to, he started looking for ministry. He discovered some people helping kids to free themselves from drugs. The workers needed more space, so he rented a building for this use and joined them in that ministry. He is involved in his own church and recently found additional temporary space for a growing youth class.

In the strength of this new life relationship, Pete found his father, whom he had vowed never to speak to again. Pete flew half way across the country to visit him, asked his forgiveness, and begged him to allow Pete to care for him as his son in his father's senior years.

Can you imagine the change in Pete? He came through Atlanta recently, and we visited at the airport. He gave me two things. One was a small rose made of thread which he sticks on the shirt lapels of his friends. It appears to be a monogram. The second gift was another book. Guess how he signed this one. That guy who once felt so unlovable that he signed "The Garbage Man" signed now in the free laughter of acceptance, knowing I could claim it with him, "One of God's Super Good Guys." Now that is good news!

Pete would be the first to acknowledge that he has not arrived, but he is on his way; he is becoming. He is beginning to taste what the writer of Ephesians called the "mature man," the "fullness of Christ." He is getting in touch with wholeness. It doesn't always happen this way, but it does happen!

Roses and monograms are not exactly my style. Someone who knows me well noticed this small rose on my lapel and kidded me about it. But I will continue to wear this rose. It represents not only an affirming brotherly friendship but also God's redemptive change in a man's life——from rubbish to roses!

What good news! It is available to each of us. We may discover it or continue it: in the ministry of God's grace to the inward person, in the outward thrust of mission, in the supportive community, in unity without uniformity, or in the process of becoming whole.

Let us go——and become!